YES,
THEY'RE
ALL OURS

RICK BOYER

Published by

THE LEARNING PARENT
Rt. 3, Box 543
Rustburg, Va. 24588

Copyright 1994

To Marilyn

her price is far above rubies

Cover Photo:

Tracey Cooter
Lynchburg, Va.

CHAPTERS

Chapter 1

YES, THEY'RE ALL OURS

I'd like you to meet my family.

Yes, they're all ours. No, we're not Catholic. No, we're not Mormon. Yes, we know what causes it. No, we don't have a television. And yes, as a matter of fact we do drive a school bus.

Marilyn and I learned years ago not to be offended by the curiosity of strangers who aren't used to seeing people out and about with twelve children. As a matter of fact, we get fewer incredulous stares now than we did when we had only half that number. People seem to just assume that we can't all be from the same family. Dining with the family one evening in a restaurant I discerned amid the hum of conversation at the table behind us a lady speculating to her companions, "Well, some of them are friends..."

The school bus was the crowning touch. We had been in need of a fifteen passenger van for a long time when my mother spotted one at a car dealership near her home in Wichita and thought immediately of us. It was a lovely thing, sleek and silver with a blue interior. And huge. Just right for the Boyers

Such a deal, the salesman assured us. The van had been owned by the school district in tiny Utica, Kansas and meticulously maintained as records in the vehicle confirmed. Out there in the sparsely populated western prairies of the

Sunflower State homes and children are few and far between so the miles on the odometer were highway miles for the most part. The van was in superb condition and they hadn't even bothered to paint it yellow. Thankfully.

To make a long story longer, I flew out, bought the van and drove it home to Virginia. Now we ride in comfort with plenty of space for everybody for the first time in years. For the benefit of the 'Whadda ya drive, a school bus?' folks we left the numeral 1 stickers on both ends of the dashboard for verification.

Meet my wife, Marilyn. Don't let her youthful looks fool you. She's a tad beyond the thirty years or so that strangers guess her age to be. And slender and beautiful though she is, that's really baby number twelve in her arms. Evidently folks assume that gestation and vitality don't go together because somebody makes the standard mistake at least once during each pregnancy: "Is this your first?" The last couple of times I had the immense pleasure of being present to see their expressions when Marilyn explained. No sound but chins hitting the floor and flies buzzing in and out of open mouths. I have occasionally been called upon to show a family photo for evidence. Nowadays Marilyn carries one in a little flat plastic case on her key ring.

Beauty is said to be only skin deep but in a virtuous woman it goes clear to the bone. My sweet little wife is adored by her family and admired by others. She is intelligent, caring, dedicated and so many other agreeable things that I can't help feeling sorry for any man who isn't married to someone just like her. Marilyn is such an excellent parent and teacher to her children that I have to go out of town on speaking engagements to get any recognition. In our community I'm known as Mr. Marilyn Boyer.

The mild annoyance of my wife's good example is atoned for by such consolations as her nutty sense of humor.

My choice jokes, guaranteed to amuse the most impassive listener, incite her only to yawn. Yet she laughs to tears over silly, simple things. She can laugh at herself when the occasion calls for it or laugh at me in such a way that I can't help laughing too. She finds it particularly entertaining when I trip and nearly fall or do something really stupid. Once she was altering some pants for me and told me to put them on backwards. She meant inside out of course, but backwards was the word she used. I thought the instructions very strange but I know nothing about sewing so I complied. When I reappeared with back pockets in front she was instantly reduced to hysterics. While trying to decide whether to call the rescue squad to resuscitate her I protested that I had only followed her instructions. She didn't hear me.

In addition to a degree of humility Marilyn has given me twelve wonderful children (aren't all your children wonderful?) who will bear introducing individually.

Rickey is our eldest at nineteen. His first interest is politics as are his second, third and fourth interests. Food might place a distant fifth. Rickey took an early interest in history and government. When he was six years old he read the fourth grade A Beka history book and liked it so much that he read it again and again for a total of eight times cover to cover during the space of his first grade year. By the time he was in his early teens he was receiving political magazines and newsletters and amazing everybody with his knowledge of current events. Today he knows more about what's going on in government than I ever hope to know. He has been involved in a number of campaigns and his career goal is to be a U.S. senator. Rick is frequently called on by our adult friends for advice on how to vote. He is most enthusiastic about those candidates whose American Conservative Union rating is one hundred per cent or higher. After a few years of working in various political campaigns as a volunteer, our son made Virginia history last fall when he was elected chairman of the Campbell County Republican Party, the youngest unit chairman in the state at present and possibly ever. Now I'm known as Mr. Marilyn Boyer locally and Rick's father What's-His-Name everywhere else in Virginia.

I can't complain. Rick has been a strong right arm to me in more ways than one. He is a help in our family ministry, works in the family business when he's not tied up with politics and has been a second father to our younger children. It's a family joke that when the Boyer babies learn to talk they start out calling me Grandpa because they think Rickey is their daddy.

Rickey was an easy baby and toddler, so God gave us Tim next to keep us humble. From the beginning Tim was Mister Mischief in our family and a veritable cornucopia of surprises. One of his early amusements was to stand on the inflated wall of Rickey's wading pool and giggle while the water ran out and his brother shrieked. Since younger siblings have come along, Tim has alternated between giving them horsie rides in his best big brotherly style and chasing them around the house growling and snarling like a lion or mad dog.

Tim at eighteen is our hands-on boy. His career goal of farming seems to arise from his love for the outdoors, animals and machines. He likes to work with his hands and seems to have a gift for anything mechanical. He helps Marilyn so much by doing home repairs that she says every family should have a Tim. I agree. Most of the time.

Nathan is now sixteen though it doesn't seem possible. Nate is a big, solid guy with a gentle spirit. Our little girls all love him and it's not uncommon for one of them to crawl up on his lap just to be there. For years we thought Nathan would grow up to be a veterinarian because he loves animals so much but lately he's talking as if he's picking up Rickey's infection with politics. He's very concerned about the ungodly direction our country has taken and seems to be reconsidering a future in veterinary work to enter the lists in government .

You'll recognize fourteen-year-old Joshua by his grin. When Josh was a baby we ironically nicknamed him Sweetness (properly pronounced Schweetness) because he was terribly fussy, particularly in church and restaurants. But at an early age his face was permanently scarred with a smile and I've seen him so tickled by nothing at all that he was incapacitated with giggles. Josh is long and lanky and determinedly progressing from just a kid to a bon a fide teenager. Like his brothers he's a good learner and an all-around guy who hopes to be a farmer someday.

Finally we did get a girl. Katie is now twelve, with long, wavy red hair that gets a lot of attention. I had anticipated that when we got a daughter to Kate's age Marilyn's housework would dwindle to nothing. Guess again. While Kate loves to cook, she sometimes forgets that the cleanup is part of the process and the kitchen ends up looking like the set of a postwar plantation scene in Gone With The Wind. Her products still show room for improvement too. She recently produced two consecutive installments of butterscotch brownies that her brothers wouldn't eat and the dog couldn't keep down.

Kate is a writer. I don't mean that in the professional sense of course, but she writes a lot. In fact by comparison she doesn't do much else. Kate writes all day and half the night, mostly producing stories. Her desk, her bed, her carpet are usually covered with sheets of paper she has filled with her work. She wanted a calligraphy book and since taking that up she's made a dollar now and then by doing calligraphy for some of the people in our church. Last year we got her some art lessons so now of course she serves as her own illustrator. Just this morning I walked out of my basement office and into the family room to find Kate sprawled across the end of the ping-pong table on her belly, one foot on the floor and one in mid-air, scratching away in a spiral notebook. Natural habitat.

Don't let a visit to our house go by without making the acquaintance of our almost youngest boy, Matthew. We nicknamed Matt Boomie early in life because of a funny sound he made with his lips when he was trying to learn to speak. Boom has many distinguishing characteristics but chief among them is his cuteness. He knows he's cute, too because everybody tells him so. But he takes fame in stride and maintains his modesty. Matthew is a loving, gentle soul with a round face, quick smile and a very sensitive heart. He would no doubt have been labeled LD had he gone to school because he didn't learn to read until age seven. But then he immediately took each of his reading books as he finished it and worked through it with his younger sister, Emily and promptly taught her to read at age five. Our little boy is ten now and long gone are the days when he toddled around the house and yard in his little summer shorts with the blue hippos. Oh, what I'd give to see that again for just one day.

An early mental portrait of Emily shows a quiet little doll of a girl gazing out from behind a pacifier which has apparently sprouted from the center of her face. Today she is a pretty eight-year-old with long blonde hair and a big-toothed grin. Emmy is not as quiet as she used to be but her even temperament and willing spirit make her very easy to live with. Emmy is also a neatnik, a quality especially prized by parents of large families. She gets upset when her sisters trash her room or leave a mess somewhere for her to straighten up. She loves to be close to Mom or Dad, even to the point of standing on the rung of my chair when I'm sitting at the kitchen table talking on the phone or snacking. It can be a bit unsettling, trying to enjoy violating your diet while someone stares in your ear from a distance of three inches. This manner of Emily's is what prompted brother Nathan to nickname her The Good Pest. .

Carrie Ellen is now seven, but don't tell her pillow or her thumb. They might get the idea they're no longer needed, which is far from the truth. Marilyn calls Carrie her inside-out-upside-down-backwards girl because of her unique style of dress. This trait carries over into other mannerisms too. Marilyn's friend Mrs. Cunningham is Mrs. Hamcunnie to Carrie. An acquaintance of mine, Burt Allen, is Burp Ellen.

Carrie is a cute little thing who loves to sit on my lap and rock while sucking her thumb and sniffing that magical dirty corner of her pillowcase. Her strawberry blonde hair and blue eyes are fetching, but it's her delightful goofiness that I find to be her greatest attraction.

Now we come to Sissy. Her real name is Christa Lee but she became Sissy early on and Sissy she remains. Her brothers call her Tiger or Tige because of a cute little growl she does in play. Sissy is tiny, very small for five years old which makes it that much easier to pick her up and cuddle her or toss and tumble her around. She has straight, light brown hair which is hard to do much with since the impromptu haircut she gave herself at age two. Perhaps her most distinguishing feature is her deep, twangy voice which Granny says just "slays" her when she hears it. It slays me, too. Despite her diminutive size Sissy is a gutsy little girl who takes no nonsense from her older brothers. Christmas before last and the Christmas before that too, she charmed me by naming the characters in the manger scene and calling Joseph "Jophus." This past year she was old enough to see through my efforts to get her to say the name the cute way and insisted on pronouncing Joseph correctly. Christmas lost a little something this year for me. I miss Jophus.

Look out world, here comes Laura. This girl is real and true though sometimes hard to believe. The ultimate four-year-old, bundle of energy and one very good reason not to keep a cat in the house. I know it's mostly my fault she's a little bit spoiled and I'm struck with an occasional pang of guilt but sometimes her antics are just too entertaining to squelch. Laura's nickname is Sam. Sam's life goal is to never fall asleep at bedtime without having escaped from bed at least three times and having been driven back. For this challenging assignment we call on brother Tim. This worthy, in the form of his mad dog alter-ego hits the floor on all fours and with ferocious snarls and roars pursues the screaming incorrigible back to her bunk,. Soon she's up again; she needs a pacifier. Somebody finds one in the family room under a sofa cushion. Back to bed for five minutes then up again and once more the chase is on.

In time past one of her favorite excuses for leaving her bed used to be her bottle. Mom would protest that Sam had resolved to give up bottles when she turned three. Sam would correct her: She had said when she turned four. Mom was sure she remembered three as the year of reckoning but lets it pass for now. Some one is assigned to locate a "bobbie" and fill it with the prescribed mixture of apple juice and water. Once again Sam would return to bed and this time settle down. That is, as long as nothing unusually interesting is happening out in the living room. One would think that anyone with Sam's energy must operate on batteries. Not so. Batteries run down sometime.

Our youngest daughter is little Brittany Grace, now two years old. Gracie is a little doll and a pet of her older brothers. Like most children her age, her vocabulary is somewhat limited but she still manages to make her opinions known. Grace has an interesting habit of making things neat. When she sees a drawer or door open, she closes it. If a toy is out of its basket she puts it back in. If she finds a book open, she shuts it and puts it away if she can. If the shelf on which the book belongs is too high for her she will put the book on a lower shelf and ask for help in until someone takes the cue. She is a good-tempered little girl and easy to get along with except for Kate, who shares a bedroom with her. Katie likes to stay up to all hours writing and sleep a little later in the morning. Brittany likes the idea of early to bed, early to rise. Maybe we should separate the girls, but then again we wouldn't mind if Gracie's early rising habit would rub off on Katie. Come to think of it, Kate could use a bit of Grace's orderliness, too.

The newest member of the team is Tucker Sean. Tuckie is now eight months old and predictably a hit with his siblings. He has already figured out that big brother Rickey is much more useful than Dad and sometimes when even Mommy can't get him to sleep at night Rick will pick him up and pace around the living room to soothe him. Tuckie will then get the benefit of Rick's early fatherliness and a news report as well, since Rick usually spends the pacing time telling the rest of us what's new in the day's politics. It sometimes seems Tuck couldn't get to sleep without his evening update.

The one remaining resident of our house doesn't really require much introduction. Enough can be gleaned about a father by the way he writes about his family. Suffice it to say that the team is still growing and I look forward to seeing what the Lord will do in our lives in the future. No doubt there are many chapters yet to be written. I'm barely more than a child myself.

FAMILY SNAPSHOTS
Part I

A few years ago Rick and Tim flew to Massachusetts to spend some time with their grandparents. During the two weeks they were gone I myself had occasion to be out of town for a few days, leaving Marilyn home with seven of the nine children we had at the time. Evidently our absence was noticed because one day eight-year-old Katie looked up and said, "Mom, it's too quiet around here!"

One evening Marilyn and I were walking through the mall with some of the children. As we passed the entrance of a new chicken restaurant we saw a man in a chicken costume dancing around and waving at the children, evidently a publicity stunt for their grand opening. As we walked by, the man took a step toward three-year-old Nathan and gave a friendly wave. Nathan crowded close to me and raised his arms to be picked up.

"I don't want the big chicken to get me," he whimpered, looking over his shoulder at the man.

It was amusing, but I felt bad for the little guy too. I hastened to reassure him, "Oh, that's not a big chicken, Natie. That's just a nice man in a chicken suit."

But Nathan just clung more tightly to me and whined, "I don't want the nice man to get me!"

Chapter 2

HOW WE GOT TO BE US

Families are like individuals in that each one has its own distinct personality and even though they all have certain things in common, certain other things about your family or mine are unique to that family. And just as individual people acquire and lose certain habits, preferences, mannerisms and so forth, families also mature and change, retaining some characteristics, losing others and developing new ones as years go by. It's been fascinating to me through the years to reflect from time to time on the stages our family has gone through and some of the influences that have given us the family personality we have today.

We haven't always been weird. In our early years Marilyn and I were not easily distinguishable from most other well-intentioned young Christian couples. We wanted a happy family, some degree of financial stability and a life of usefulness to God. I wanted to live on a farm and work in a ministry. Marilyn wanted to have children and be a keeper at home. Nothing that hadn't ever been thought of before.

At the time of our marriage I was a twenty-year-old medic in the Air Force. My plan was to finish out my enlistment then move to Lynchburg, Virginia to earn a college degree in youth work, after which I expected to work as a youth director in some church. I got my youth group all right, but not the type I expected. That was one of a number of surprises that lay ahead.

The fact that Marilyn and I ever got together must have surprised some observers. She was the little princess, intelligent, well-mannered, attractive. She wore dresses to school when all the other girls and boys alike dressed in tattered, faded jeans. Member in good standing of the

12

Yes, They're All Ours

National Honor Society, pillar of the high school youth group at church.

I was the quintessential young jerk. I admit it; I had a big mouth, loved attention and was short on discretion. Not overburdened with social graces, I had grown up in Kansas where people are normal and was not hesitant to comment on the stuffiness of the residents of the Massachusetts community to which I had been transplanted by my affectionate Uncle Sam.

As they say in the romance novels, I'll never forget the night we met. I don't think Marilyn will, either. It was after church on a Sunday evening in my early days on Cape Cod.. A bunch of us young people had hung around after the service chatting and I was flopped on the carpet in my natural position which was horizontal. I had been noticing a pretty young lady with long brown hair and was wondering how I could get acquainted with her. Although I was very much outgoing among friends, I had always been extremely shy with girls whom I didn't know well. I had been on very few dates mainly because I was terrified to ask anyone out. Now here was the perfect opportunity to meet a lovely young lady in an informal setting and Bucketmouth Boyer couldn't think of any way to start a conversation.

What I finally did to get her attention was not eminently successful and I'll admit it was more the product of impulse than reflection. I waited until she walked by where I was reclining in the center aisle then reached out and grabbed her ankle.

The move could be said to have worked quite well in that it definitely got her to notice me, but her response was not all I could have desired. She gave me a look like the one you'd give to a roach just before stepping on it.

At age nineteen I was not a deep well of brilliant insight but I was perceptive enough to realize that this relationship was not off to a good start. Perhaps all was not lost, though. Maybe she was just one of those people who couldn't take a joke. No doubt she would get to know me over the course of time and be able to discern the many fine character qualities she had missed at first glance.

It did take some time. Asking around about her, I found out that her name was Marilyn Huebener (pronounced "Heebener" but not usually), that she was a senior in high school, very intelligent, very nice and an outstanding Christian girl.

I felt fairly safe in ruling her out as a romantic prospect. Still, as time went by her blind spots lessened to the point that she came to see that I was actually a nice guy and at least, not dangerous. She and I grew to be friends. And though I still held her in awe I liked her and eventually came to be comfortable in her presence.

One Sunday morning after the worship service I was standing in front of the church enjoying the sunshine and visiting with the folks as they spilled out the front doors and spread out across the lawn and parking lot. Marilyn Miss Perfect Huebener drifted over and stood next to me as a stream of little children, some of them her Sunday School students, poured out of the church and down the sidewalk. Marilyn adored children and would turn the loveliest shade of pink when holding someone's baby, which she seemed to do at every opportunity. Now she watched lovingly as the little ones went by. "I want kids," she sighed. Then after a second's pause she looked up at me and said with a perfectly straight face, "I'm coming to you, Rick..."

By the time they had me resuscitated it had dawned on me that mischief and a sense of humor were among the many interesting attributes of Miss Perfect.

Time went by. One day my youth group buddy, Frank and I were over at the home of the Watkins', a family in the

14

church. Mrs. Watkins, who evidently enjoyed an occasional foray into the field of matchmaking, mentioned that she had heard that that nice Marilyn Huebener was currently unattached. "Why don't one of you boys ask her out?" she suggested slyly.

"Not me," I said reverently. "She's 'way too classy for me. Why don't you ask her, Frank?"

"Naw, too classy for me, too," he said.

But seed had been sown (not to say the thought had never before crossed my mind) and after much hemming and hawing I finally managed to wangle a date with Marilyn. We went out to dinner and I was too nervous to eat, which she thought was just terribly cute and I thought was disgusting. At least it was a start.

I hadn't been eager to meet Marilyn's parents. Massachusetts isn't Mississippi, and people don't throw their arms around you and call you Honey at the first introduction. (Marilyn's father had always told her not to date GI's. Now she knows why, but it's too late.) When I came to pick their daughter up that first time, Marilyn's mother and sister were polite as if willing to give me a chance. When Marilyn introduced me to her father, he was sitting in a living room chair that faced half away from us as we walked in and stood beside it.

"Dad, this is Rick Boyer. Rick, this is my dad."

"Pleased to meet you, sir," I said, standing almost at attention.

"Hnh."

Oh.

Marilyn's dad and I are buddies now that he's had a few years of beating me at lawn darts. He's really a good guy. Just hesitant to show it prematurely.

Never having been one to rush a relationship, I waited until our third date to inform Marilyn that we were going to get married. She laughed. We had just started dating, she had just finished her first semester of college and I was a rough-hewn young GI whose personal assets amounted to a negative number. However she stopped laughing in time for our wedding, which took place seven months later.

The rest, as they say, is history. We have now been married for over twenty years and I love to remind my wife of the time she said she wanted children and was coming to me for help. She came to the right place.

I think I've hinted that I was pretty raw material when Marilyn got me. Although it's not a boost to my ego, I wanted to share that fact so that hopefully it will encourage young fathers who feel inadequate that they really can start off quite ignorant and learn on the job. It may also relieve the fears of some wives who are wondering just what they've gotten themselves into.

January 3, 1972 was one of the most important days of my life. That was the day I discovered the Bible. Of course I knew the Bible existed. I owned one in addition to the New Testament that had been in my gift bag from the Salvation Army, something given to every new recruit at that time. I had been born again the summer before my senior year in high school and had been told that reading the Bible was good for me so I tried. But the King James English was too heavy for me and I never got far at all. I remember wanting to find some comfort in my New Testament during basic training and even sneaking it into my bunk with me and straining my eyes to read it by the light of the exit sign over the nearby fire escape. Later in technical school after basic I would arise at 4:30 AM to read a chapter or two before breakfast and reporting to class at six. But still the text was inscrutable to me and I never felt that I benefited much. It wasn't until a few weeks after I landed in

Massachusetts that the Lord opened my eyes and I hit pay dirt.

The People's Republic of Massachusetts was no place for a hillbilly boy to feel at home but let's give credit where credit is due. It's not all funny accents and snobbery up there. While my personal opinion is that they go to extremes with their emphasis on academics and education (you can't get a job as dog catcher without a Master's degree), there was a benefit that resulted from the spillover of this attitude in the church. The church I attended there was much different from the one in which I became a Christian as a high school boy in Kansas. In my home church the theme had been along the lines of motivation with an emphasis on salvation. The Massachusetts church was heavy on instruction in the Scriptures, which was exactly what I needed at that stage in my life. It's funny how these coincidences happen.

I had been on Cape Cod just a few weeks when I had a conversation at the back of the auditorium one evening with Pastor Hansen and Mrs. Clark, the lady who with her husband headed up the youth group and was a surrogate mom to a number of young people, me included. I had heard the term "growth" used so many times in reference to spiritual development that I had finally begun to suspect that there was more to the Christian life than I had learned thus far. In the time of informal after-service fellowship I had cornered Pastor Hansen.

"What is this business of spiritual growth?" I asked him. "I've heard it mentioned a number of times since I came here, but what does it mean? How do you grow spiritually?"

P.H. was and is a motivated teacher and he jumped on that question like a duck on a June bug.

"Well, Rick, what would your physical health be like if you didn't take in enough food? You'd be weak, you

17

wouldn't function well, you wouldn't have such good skin coloring..." My rosy-cheeked youth was then upon me, you see. The reverend continued.

"The Bible is our spiritual food. When we eat right as Christians, we grow and develop as we should. Most Christians neglect their Bibles and that's why they don't grow beyond the baby stage."

Mrs. Clark had joined us and now chimed in.

"It sounds trite, Rick, but read your Bible and pray," she exhorted me.

"That's not trite," I assured her. "Nobody ever told me that before."

I left church that night determined to give this spiritual growth business a fair try. But again the King James English stymied me. I had, after all, been reared by a public school and a television set. I wasn't a test tube baby, I was a picture tube baby.

This took place just before Christmas I believe and the big breakthrough came just after the beginning of the new year. January third was my first day back at work after the Christmas break. It was also a turning point for me in more ways than one. I was about to be crosstrained from my original job which was in the military police to the medical career field. In the meantime I was assigned to work at the K-9 section babysitting the dogs. My schedule was easy. When I first arrived in the morning I fed the dogs then picked up the pans and washed them. Next I cleaned the kennels. All this took an hour and a half or so, then I had practically nothing to do until I gave the kennels another quick cleaning just before going off duty.

During the several hours' interim I had a lot of free time so I brought some reading with me in the form of the New Testament in paraphrase form, a Christmas gift from some church friends. That day for the first time I felt I could understand the Bible. I sat down and started reading and went on until time for the afternoon scoop session. Allowing for interruptions and a thirty-minute lunch break I read the Bible for five hours that day.

This is perhaps no cause for astonishment to a lot of people who have been students of the Scriptures for years, but for me it was revolutionary. Not only had I learned from what I read, but there was something else, a feeling inside as of batteries that had received their first electrical charge. It was deeper than just the encouragement of finally beginning to understand intellectually; I had somehow made connection to the Source of spiritual strength. As I left the building after work that day I felt as I had never felt before. Throughout the rest of the month I averaged about three hours of Bible reading per day. On February 1st I completed the New Testament for the first time, a feat which would have seemed a year's work to me before.

It was at the very end of 1972 that Marilyn and I started dating. I wasn't much but at least I had had a year under the influence of daily Scripture reading. And though I was still a confused, unhappy youth, lonely and bored while far from home in a foreign land, I had discovered a power that was changing me day by day. My new wife and I had a long way to go but we were learning that the Bible is the road map.

It was on our honeymoon that the differences between her breeding and mine began to surface. We had a real country honeymoon in the Ozarks including creek fishing, cliff diving at Table Rock Lake and best of all, staying for a few days at my Grandparents' farm. Grandad had always been my favorite relative. He was a genuine old time hillbilly farmer who wore bib overalls, plowed his garden with a horse, played the country fiddle and enjoyed fox hunting with his hounds. These canines were not your sissified city dogs, but rather tough, stringy, long-winded harriers who could chase a fox all night long through the rough, rocky briar patches and thickets of the southwestern Missouri hills and then beg for more at sundown the next day.

Grandad's dogs weren't fashion plates, either. They were generally skinny, footsore, smelly and covered with ticks. It was not the refined canine life Hollywood stars gave to their dogs. Marilyn and I had bought an Irish Setter puppy in the course of our postnuptial travels and the first evening at Grandad's, I was preparing to settle the pup down in the barn for the night. Marilyn was horrified. The barn was dirty and the baby would cry with loneliness, she protested.

"Leave one o' yer shoes out there with her," Grandad advised. "She won't holler as much."

"Couldn't we keep her in the house with us?" Marilyn asked me.

Grandad answered for me. "Why, shore," he assured her with a grin, "I always bring my fox dogs in to sleep with me!"

Grandad never in his life had indoor plumbing. He got his water the way real men do, with a rope and pulley above the well and a bucket and dipper on the counter just inside the back door. He had a genuine outhouse too, a two-seater with a tin roof and painted barn red. Classic.

My new bride was Bostonian by birth and all this quaint charm was absolutely wasted on her. In the middle of the night I woke up to the sound of her crying. Marilyn cries very quietly and at first I didn't know what was going on. Finally I understood and asked sleepily what was wrong.

"I have to go to the bathroom," she sniffled.

"So go," I said, confused. "What's the problem?"

"It's *outside*!"

They say all marriages involve adjustments and that the first fifty years are the hardest. We both survived our honeymoon, but it wasn't the period of ecstasy they write

20

about in the glossy paperbacks. In fact the first year was pretty miserable in some ways. We had only been back from our honeymoon for a few weeks when I was shipped out to Florida for my final months in the military. We never really felt at home in Florida. Marilyn, who had been extremely busy with college and wedding preparations in the months preceding our marriage now found herself stuck in an apartment all day with nothing to do, no money, no transportation and surrounded by strangers instead of the family and friends near whom she had lived all her life. Since I had to have our one car to get to work every day there was no way for her to even take a job to pass the time. It was probably a good thing that we didn't have a television. Marilyn had never watched much TV but with so much time on her hands it could have been a problem. As it was, we both got used to not having one around and we haven't owned a television since (other than one that was given to us with a computer to serve as a monitor).

Marilyn wasn't alone in misery that year. I hated my new job in the base hospital, we couldn't find a church where we were comfortable (mostly because of my immature attitudes) and we never developed much of a circle of friends. Marilyn probably wondered if she had done the right thing by getting married. I wondered if I had done the right thing by being born.

Finally the awful fourteen months were over. That was in 1974 and the military was reducing forces after having withdrawn from Viet Nam the year before. The Air Force was offering early discharges to many personnel who were nearing the end of their enlistment and I wasted no time applying for one. Prior to receiving the news of this program, I had been interviewed by my boss, Sgt. Paul Beal concerning my plans.

21

"Rick, I've got this form I need to fill out on you. It's something the Air Force does in order to project their future manpower needs."

He asked me a number of questions but only one sticks in my mind: "What are your interests and intentions concerning the Air Force?" .

"My interest is in getting out and my intention is to do so at the earliest opportunity."

He grinned. "That the way you want me to write it down?"

"Write it down just like that."

Somebody must have taken the hint because I was one of the fortunate ones who received an early release a few months later. My last day in the service I was walking on air. I had finished with my regular duties and was just going through processing for discharge. I had appointments at the personnel office, finance office, medical evaluations and some other exciting events which for some reason slip my mind right now. Marilyn and I had packed a rented U-Haul trailer with our few possessions the evening before and so when my processing was finished and I had said goodbye to all my on-base friends nothing remained but an evening engagement with a family from our church. Next morning we headed up the highway toward Virginia and a couple of days later I found myself in Lynchburg in time for the winter semester with a wife, a month-old baby, two big dogs and twenty-eight dollars to my name. It hadn't been an easy move, but it was another sterling performance in a long line of brilliant successes.

It will be easiest on my conscience to fast-forward through the next few months. We were living in a mobile home park, I was in college and making ends meet (sort of) between my GI Bill benefits and whatever part-time work I could find. Life was tough because we were still trying to learn our roles as marriage partners and parents. For me the role of breadwinner had suddenly become complicated without Uncle Sam there to tell me every move to make and supply me with a steady paycheck. I found in fact that it was very nerve-wracking to balance working, college and family life. My career in the hallowed halls lasted from January 1975 through summer school. I dropped out, fumbled with more part-time work for a while and in the fall took a job with the prison system. I was now no longer a high school boy, a young GI, a college student or a bachelor. I had a wife, a baby boy (Rickey had been born a month before my discharge from the Air Force) and a full-time job. For the first time in my life I had entered the real world and I found that my education was just beginning.

One of the foundation stones of that education had been laid in the early weeks of my marriage. Marilyn and I had visited a Christian book store, something I had never done before. We both wanted to learn more about the Christian life but were unsure as to how to go about it. We hoped to find some commentary or something that would help us understand the Bible better and maybe some useful books on Christian living. One book we bought was better than either one. It was Young's Concordance.

The only concordance I knew about was the few pages of alphabetical listings in the back of some Bibles. Unfortunately, I usually couldn't do much with one of those, since they never seemed to contain a reference to the verse I was looking for or more than a few verses on any one topic. When we found Young's we felt that we had discovered a gold mine, which in fact we had. As we stood there flipping through it I said, "Exhaustive? Does that mean this thing lists every verse in the whole Bible?"

"I guess it does," Marilyn answered.

"Then I can look up any topic I want to know about and find out what the Bible says about it?"

"Looks like it."

We looked at each other wide-eyed. We felt like shouting "Eureka!" or something of the sort, but the atmosphere in the Christian bookstore wasn't all that conducive. Instead we bought the concordance and a couple of other books and walked quietly out.

The discovery that we, lay persons without Bible college training, could do our own research and find out what God says about any subject in which we were interested was revolutionary. Looking back it's hard to believe we were so ignorant, but neither of us had grown up in homes where the Bible was an important part of the family frame of reference. We have never been the Bible students we should be, but we have learned to let our fingers do the walking. This has been important especially when we have had a decision to make and were unsure that our own inclinations or the advice we were hearing were right. We've come to believe that if Christian families would search the Scriptures on a subject before making major decisions, many people would be living differently.

One such subject became a topic of study to us and another major milestone in our life. It was when I was in college that winter semester. I was taking a course called Christian Ethics and I was regularly impressed that my professor would document every topic he addressed by giving Scripture references that highlighted what God had to say on the subject. It was when he turned to the topic of birth control that I really woke up.

He started out by quoting Scriptures that said children are a blessing. He made a very strong case that God wants to give most families several children. He gave me the strong impression that he himself believed in letting God plan family size. Then he began to talk about exceptions to the rule and there my antennae went up.

This professor had previously been a pastor and he told us about a woman who had come to him for counsel concerning birth control. She had five children who were wild and unruly and she was pulling her hair out. Would it be wrong, she asked, to limit her family to those five?

"I okayed it in her case because they really were driving her crazy," he said.

That immediately struck a discordant note with me. In my military police days I had worked with police dogs and I knew that dogs can be trained to obey and not drive their handlers crazy. My one son was still an infant but I saw no reason that children couldn't be trained to behave as well. Besides, I had grown up in a family where it had been made known that consistently unruly behavior would bring dire consequences. Why wasn't this pastor advising this woman on how to train her children instead of just limiting their number? And, having built a strong Biblical case for letting God plan the family, where were the Scriptures for this exception?

Back to the concordance I went, looking for verses on children and parenthood. I found a number of references and the consistent theme was that children are a blessing. Psalm 127 even called them a gift from God. Nowhere could I find an example of someone who had committed some vile sin and been punished with parenthood. No scenes of Elijah preaching out thunder: "Oh, so you want to worship idols, huh? Well, God's gonna curse you with children and children's children! Take that!"

Another thing I noticed is that God is the One Whose role it is to open and close the womb. There were instances of His closing the womb in judgment and opening the womb as a reward, but never the reverse. Marilyn and I came to the conclusion that we would rather let God make the choice than take such a responsibility upon ourselves. We don't try to force our conclusion on others, but it seems a shame that Christians as a rule are horrified by abortion and yet treat conception so casually.

As we thought about all this we were struck with sadness that we hadn't started our marriage with the assumption that God would give us children at the right time without coaching from us. We had been planning to wait on children because that's what everybody did. We really didn't know what we were waiting for or how long we were waiting, we were just waiting. In the meantime, Marilyn was spending her days in loneliness and boredom with no company but a hard-headed Irish Setter. Our fourteen months in Florida were horrible for Marilyn except for the last month when she had Rickey and then her life was transformed.

The year following my entry into full-fledged adult life brought a couple more major changes as we acquired a second baby boy and bought our first home. We were still poor as church mice and never could seem to get a car that had all four wheels going the same direction, but if I had known then what I know now I would have been much more content. It was a good, simple, wholesome life and if only I hadn't still had so much to learn frustrations would have been minimal. But you know how young fellows are. I couldn't see the progress I wanted toward making something important of my life, not being wise enough to understand that working a job, rearing children and making a wife happy are superb training for spiritual leadership. So I spent a lot of time on edge wishing something was different but not knowing exactly what. I've often said that if God has a hobby it's watching young men squirm.

The next few years saw the entry of two more Boyer boys and the beginning of formal education for Rickey and

Yes, They're All Ours

Timmy. We knew this latter was a turning point in our family's life but had no idea how revolutionary it would turn out to be.

We discovered home education by accident, or so it seemed. When Rick and Tim were four and three years old respectively, we sent them to our church's excellent preschool program. There were only a handful of boys and girls in preschool as our church was small and we enrolled only children of members for the most part. There were two and sometimes three adults working with the children and the training was very much spiritually oriented. We loved the things that were being taught and the wise, loving way the teachers treated the little people. We had no objection whatever to what was going on with Rick and Tim. It was what Nathan and Joshua were enduring that made us change direction.

I was in the bathtub one evening soaking out the kinks my body had collected during the day. Marilyn came in to talk (Henny Youngman used to say he wished his wife would stay out of the bathroom when he was in the tub because she was so immature. She couldn't resist the urge to sink all his boats). My wife took a seat somewhere and said she had something on her mind.

"What would you think about my teaching Rickey kindergarten at home next year?" she asked.

I gave my standard reply to unexpected questions.

"Huh?"

"I'm wondering if I could keep the boys home next year and teach Rickey kindergarten myself. What do you think?"

It should be remembered that this took place back when I was young, approximately the same year the Ark landed. I had never heard of home education other than in the case of Abraham Lincoln.

"Why do that instead of sending the boys back to school? We've got a fantastic school."

"I know, " she said. "It's getting them there that's the problem."

She went on to explain the problems of commuting. Although we were able to carpool to a limited extent, Marily was the school bus driver for our boys most of the time. The trip to school was made three times a week. Rick and Tim attended half days on Monday and Wednesday, Rick alone on Friday. So three days each week Marilyn buckled the boys into their car seats and made an hour-long round trip to drop off Rick and Tim.

It was tiny Nathan and Josh who suffered most. They spent two hours each day strapped in their seats so that their brothers could have four hours in school. And I could see how Marilyn would chafe at all the wasted time. She's very efficient and would much rather be home with her children than out running around town. The situation really chopped the day up for everybody.

The idea of home education caught me off-guard but it wasn't hard to get used to. Marilyn had been an education major in college with the intention of being an elementary school teacher before she threw her life away and married me. She had done considerable student teaching while in high school and had been an excellent student herself. She had squeezed two years' college credit into one year's time (I squeezed two years' credit into eight years' time) and the superintendent of schools in her home town had told her before she left for college that she would have a teaching job waiting for her when she finished. There was no doubt she had the ability. And after all, it was just for kindergarten.

After a consultation with our school's administrator who assured us we could handle it, we finalized our decision. It turned out to be life-changing.

Yes, They're All Ours

Fall came and Marilyn began to teach Rickey from books we had obtained through the school. It wasn't long before we decided to keep him at home for first grade as well. By the time the year was over we saw no need to send him to school ever. Rickey is nineteen now and he's never even gone to high school except for one day last fall. After he got elected county chairman of his political party he was asked to come to a local school and lecture the senior government class.

As I said, we had never heard of the home education movement at the time we started. As far as we know we were the only family home teaching in our area at the time. The next year some friends of ours started, then the next year there were nine families. The following year there were about thirty-five and a support group was started. The year after that we had about ninety families and after that we lost count. In 1984 Virginia passed new provisions in the compulsory attendance statute that made home education much easier legally and now there are hundreds of families home educating in our three-county area.

Because we were among the first in the state to start home teaching we received a lot of requests for information and occasionally were asked to speak to a local support group. Later our state organization began to have yearly conventions and one or both of us usually do workshops at those. In recent years we've developed The Learning Parent seminar on Christian Home Education, written a regular column in the *Home School Digest* magazine and authored four books. Because I still have to operate a separate business to make a living, our work for home educators gets pretty demanding. But to see young parents make the decision to teach their own children, to speak to groups of them and see their faces light up with encouragement when I share with them our early struggles and the many rewards, makes it well worth the trouble. They do much more for me than I do for them. They are my heroes.

FAMILY SNAPSHOTS
Part II

It was late on a cold and snowy winter night that I was awakened by my dog's insistent barking. The family had had a full and busy day; snowstorms aren't frequent in our part of Virginia and one that dumps enough snow to play in is always welcome. To the children, that is.

On this particular day, the boys had enjoyed the white stuff to the fullest. There had been rides on the toboggan courtesy of Daisy Belle, my faithful Bloodhound who didn't mind being harnessed to the sled as long as she had me running alongside for company. We'd enjoyed snowball fights, built a snowman and eaten snow ice cream. Bedtime had come and we had all been ready.

But now my sleep was interrupted by Daisy with her barking. And it wasn't normal barking. Daisy had different tones of voice for a variety of occasions and I could usually tell right away whether she was challenging another dog, a human intruder, or trying to get the attention of someone in the house to order room service. This bark, delivered in the funny, baying tones of the Bloodhound sounded like her people bark but something was different. I lay listening for a minute trying to wake up enough to figure it out. What was she doing out of her kennel behind the storage shed? And what was that strange note of doubt in her bark? She sounded uncertain somehow, not quite confident as she usually was when she accosted a stranger. The direction from which the sound came was wrong as well. I heard her in the back yard, then I heard her from the driveway at the end of the house. Then the bark came from the back yard again, then once more from the driveway.

31

I was working as a deputy sheriff at the time and because of the nature of my job I tended to be a bit jumpy. I had seen a lot of mayhem and had my life threatened a few times. I quickly left the bed, donned pants and took my service revolver from its shelf in the closet. Then, tiptoeing quickly through the dark house I made my way to the kitchen from which windows overlooked both the driveway and the back yard. Again Daisy barked from the driveway and looking out I could see her dark form clearly against the moonlit snow. Then she disappeared around the corner of the house and gave her hesitant bark once more. Instantly she appeared once again in the driveway and again came the strange, doubtful challenge.

By now I was satisfied that my dog was indeed barking at a person and that the person was behind and quite close to my house. As quietly as possible I opened the side door and stepped out onto the snowy porch. I took a deep breath, readied my weapon and suddenly jumped around the corner of the house. There in the middle of the moonlit yard stood the man who had aroused my dog's protective instincts. A large man, heavy set and awkward looking, he stood silent and unmoving in the icy night air. In an instant I was around the corner and confronting him. My pistol braced in both hands, I started to yell *"Freeze!"* but the shout died on my lips as I realized he was already frozen. It was the snowman.

Daisy Belle, escape artist extraordinaire, had been in her pen that afternoon while the boys had been engaged in snowman construction. True to form, she had waited until the household was asleep to make her clandestine exit for a little late night stroll and had been unaware of the snowman's presence until she rounded the corner of the shed and saw him. No doubt she started barking instantly, but she was put off balance by the fact that although she saw a man, all she smelled was snow. Bloodhounds are known for their powerful sense of smell and it must have been unnerving for Daisy to see a man scant yards away and not be able to catch a trace of scent from him. No wonder her usual confidence had been absent from her bark.

Wearily I returned my dog to her kennel and headed back to my bed, musing as I did so that while the keenness of the Bloodhound's nose is legendary, I've never heard anyone brag much about their brains.

Chapter 3

LIFE IN THE BIG FISHBOWL

You can't expect life to be easy when you have so many children that Planned Parenthood is considering you for next year's poster child.

One of the facts of life in the large family is that when you're out and about with your brood you're not going to be able to sneak up on anybody. If we had names for our five vehicles I'd call the passenger van Exodus. That's the idea that comes to mind whenever we go someplace en masse.

Over the years we've encountered some interesting reactions from people. Some just stare. Others try to stare inconspicuously. Many ask, "Are these all *your* children?" It's wonderful when we have only eight or nine present and we can say, "Oh no, these aren't all our children." We wait for their sigh of relief before adding, "We have three more at home!"

Some clever comebacks have been suggested to us for use with inquirers, but I'd hate to seem disrespectful to anybody. The overwhelming majority of those who ask about it mean no harm and in fact most act approving, even admiring.

One common remark is, "I don't know how you can stand it. I wouldn't have the patience."

I usually answer that patience grows. I wouldn't have wanted to get my twelve all at the same time.

Another frequent comment: "My, you have your hands full!"

Answer: (With a respectful smile) "Yes, and they used to be empty."

To the friendly, funloving type who asks, "Wow! Twelve! Are you Catholic, Mormon or crazy?"

34

"No, we're not Catholic, no we're not Mormon, and no, we're not crazy. Yet. But we're making progress."

One of the funniest reactions I've seen was when we walked into a restaurant one evening with our children, who at that time numbered only five. A lady sitting directly across the dining room stared at us as we trooped in. She could have been a character in a television comedy. We were too far away to hear her whisper if in fact she made any sound at all, but I could read her lips plainly as she stared and counted: *"One, two, three, four, five!"* Then she pulled her fascinated eyes away from us for an instant to whisper to her friend at the table and again I heard no sound but could read her lips easily. *"Five kids?!"*

Big deal. She acted as if she'd seen somebody out walking five Rottweilers.

One time our family size really paid off. We were dining out after church one Sunday afternoon and a well-dressed gentleman at a nearby table stopped by to compliment us on our children's behavior. Our children aren't perfect, you understand. We all have our days. And I'm sure lots of small families have well-behaved children too. But when you have a family the size of ours people pay attention. And they notice the children's behavior, too, whether it's good or bad.

This was a good day and as we were leaving the restaurant we got several approving smiles. Arriving at the checkout counter to pay my bill, I was nudged by somebody. It was the kind gentleman who had said nice things about my kids. He asked for my ticket and said he'd like to pay for our meal. Why? He just wanted to, he said. Then he corrected himself. He thought the Lord wanted him to.

Who was I to argue with the Lord? Having a large family entails all kinds of side benefits.

Speaking of benefits, we've been offered some we elected to turn down. Once Marilyn had to sit waiting in line somewhere and she was chatting with the lady next to her, who happened to be employed by the welfare department. The lady asked how many children Marilyn had, to which my wife replied that she was the mother of eight.

"Eight children," exclaimed the lady, her eyes widening. "Why, honey, you ought to come down and see us. You're eligible for everything we've got!"

One gratifying remark by an observer came to us through the manager of the same restaurant where we enjoyed the free meal I mentioned earlier. He stopped to chat with Marilyn and me when we were out by ourselves one evening.

"You know, we get a lot of positive comments from other customers about your kids."

We didn't interrupt. Hopefully he'd say more.

"Last time you were in with the kids there was a state policeman sitting pretty close to you."

We remembered. The manager continued,

"He left right behind you and as he and I watched you go out he said to me, 'There go some kids I'll never deal with on the job.'"

Not everybody appreciates us. The occasional sourpuss along the way has looked us over, decided we were in fact one family and given us a wide berth and a last glance of utter disdain. They seem to view a large family as an oversize litter of mongrel puppies.

One lady who has become a dear friend of ours confessed that when we first met she thought we were crazy. Fortunately she saw at least some things in our children that she appreciated and her attitude mellowed over the years. That's not the only time such a thing has happened, but she was frank enough to say it out loud. Others are not always so open. A friend of ours joined a church in which we had once been members. She could, I'm sure sit for hours and tell us things she's heard about us both positive and negative and some even fabricated. Once she made the mistake of mentioning us as an example of a healthy family and a lady present jumped on her: "Why, they can't afford all those children! They've taken bankruptcy!" I don't know where she got her false information, but some people seem to make some pretty strong assumptions. I know of a lady who now seems to like us fairly well but when she first heard of us responded with, "Nobody has a right to have that many children! It's my tax money that's paying for all that welfare!"

Some people see us as trailblazers. One friend whose children are younger than ours said, "I sure am glad you guys are going through all this before I have to." At your service.

We've been called the grandparents of the home education movement in our area because we have helped a number of families to get started who now in turn have assisted a lot of other families. We were doing it first, we did it with a large number of children first, we went to court first. I'd just as soon have skipped the court part. It used to displease me to be addressed as grandparent of the local movement. I wasn't nearly old enough to be anybody's grandfather. Nowadays it doesn't bother me particularly because I am nearly old enough. Though of course you could never tell it.

Sometimes it's a burden to be watched so much, but the appreciation we receive from those who glean encouragement from what we say and do is a great compensation. One dear lady at a state convention heard

Marilyn speak about home educating the large family and at the end of the workshop stood up to give a testimony. She said that she was pregnant with her fourth child and that she had decided prior to hearing Marilyn that she would have her tubes tied and make her fourth her last. She loved children and felt they were truly a blessing, but she was getting so much criticism from family and friends that she felt she had reached the limit of her endurance. Now, however, she felt that she would be wrong to take that decision into her own hands. With tears in her eyes (and just possibly in a few other eyes as well) she shared that she was committing the decision as to the size of her family, to the Lord. She concluded by saying that when she came into the room in which the workshop was held she hadn't really known what made her choose that workshop over the other ones available at the same time. Now, she said, she knew. Just goes to show that one should use caution in deciding to hear Marilyn Boyer speak.

I'm sure we're an irritation to some with our opinions and ideas. We try to be discreet, but there are some things that are obvious and the desire for a large family can't be kept secret for long. At the same time, our lifestyle can occasionally be an encouragement. In working with home educators and prospective home educators our struggles often serve to reassure the fainthearted that they can indeed handle the challenges. If we can do it, they can do it too. For example:

Q: How can we home educate? Neither of us has a
   college degree.
A: Neither do my wife or I.

Q: How can we home educate? We've never done anything like that.

A: When we started, we didn't even know anybody was doing it.

Q: How can we home educate? I need my wife's income from her job.

A: Learn to manage. When our ninth child was born I was earning less than 25K a year.

Q: How can we home educate? Everybody will think we're weird.

A: Everybody is sure we're weird.

Q: How can we home educate? We have too many children to get organized.

A: Heh, heh, heh.

One of the interesting things we've learned in having a big family is the number of prejudices people have about the subject. For instance, Marilyn has found that people respond differently to a baby depending upon its location, whether inside or outside of her tummy. She says that if some lady sees her in the grocery store with a tiny baby and asks her how many children she has the questioner more often will respond with a combination of surprise and approval. If Marilyn is still pregnant however, and is asked "what number" the new little one will be, she often gets looks of shock and distaste. Now 'splain that one to me. After all, Marilyn always wears shoes in the grocery store.

I once saw a Dear Abby column (no, I'm not a regular reader) that had as a theme the idea that women who have large families are loonies. Several different letters took prolific mamas to task, accusing them of everything from having children just to get attention (there must be an easier way to get attention) to being insecure and producing babies repeatedly so they can feel needed. Don't know if anybody really does it for the latter reason, but if they do I'll bet it works.

Life in the big fishbowl has had ramifications for us that I would not have expected. Some people seem to be watching in the hope of seeing one of our children go to jail for shoplifting (They may be disappointed to learn that Ruth down at the corner store says our kids are the only ones in the neighborhood she doesn't watch like a hawk every minute they're in the building. Others view us just as a curiosity and check in now and then to see what's (or who's) new. And then are those blessed people some of whom I've already mentioned, who think we're wonderful because we're doing something they wish they dared to do.

In a gathering at the home of friends the other evening a couple of people reminded us that they had been watching us for years in anticipation of seeing our unpopular views vindicated. They are part of a kind of cheering section we have rooting for us. I think many people who know us understand a little about the pressures we've experienced over the years in the process of bucking the social tide.

Apart from the idea of having all the children God chooses to send and giving them their basic education at home, there are side issues concerning which people watch us. Career preparation is one such thing. Somebody told us recently that they're eagerly watching our son Rick as he moves up in the arena of politics. So many have challenged us on our ability to put twelve children through college that our sympathizers can't wait to see Rickey reach the Senate without ever taking a college class. I think a lot of people are tired of the standard dogmas of our day: Fewer children is better, you can't succeed without college, parents aren't capable of teaching, the nuclear family is a defunct institution, children may be forced to obey but they have to make all their own mistakes, it's natural for adolescents to rebel, Proverbs 22:6 just means they'll always come back (that's a pretty far cry from not departing), women need careers to be fulfilled, etc. And there are those who are tired of those godless lies but are either not so situated as to personally demonstrate their falsehood (like some of your friends who are not able to have any more babies) or who just haven't quite mustered the audacity to take the plunge as yet. They may be unequipped or unprepared but for many of them I can say they're on our side. I hope we've let the cheerleaders in our life know that we appreciate them deeply. I also hope those who read this and wonder if the large family lifestyle is for them, will consider it prayerfully. If there is one thing our country desperately needs it is the example of people who treasure children and I can personally testify that there are great compensations for the resistance you will face. One is the support of those who cannot do what you can do but look to you to wear their colors, those who stand outside the fishbowl and pray.

FAMILY SNAPSHOTS
Part III

Innocent Emily and mischievous Tim make an interesting combination. Tim developed a special voice for addressing Emmy when he was in a playful mood. There's no way to reproduce it in print but it was distorted, half-intelligible, a combination of mocking, scolding and general derision. No human ear could decipher most of the tirade that poured forth when Tim was in character, but the name Pec kept recurring amid the flow. He had seen a picture of a peccary in a book and told Emmy that's what she was. The *piece de resistance* of the routine was his laugh. This grossly exaggerated and distorted caricature of a laugh was a mixture of laugh, cough and dry heaves. As he pretended to laugh he made it more ridiculous by hanging his tongue out to an impossible length A single laugh, delivered with arm outstretched and finger pointed at the victim, the other hand held tight against Tim's chest as if holding his belly in a fit of merriment and yet so patently false that...well, you just have to see it.

Sometimes Emmy would try to kick her brother in the shins and, failing, walk away in a huff. When his antics would really get under her skin she'd start weeping with rage and shout for her mother, "Mommy! Timmy's laughing at me!!"

One day Emmy, age three, did something that inspired Tim to go into his act. He berated her for a minute in his bizarre voice, then broke the camel's back with his patented laugh. Emmy was in no mood for it. "Mommy!" she screamed, "Timmy's laughing at me!"

Whirling away from her antagonist, the little lady stormed out the front door while Tim walked away grinning. But no sooner had Emmy slammed the door behind her than she caught sight of Bonnie, our dog lying in the flower bed seeking relief from the heat in the cool dirt. She had her canine air conditioner running, mouth wide open in a doggy grin, ivory teeth showing and long, dripping tongue hanging nearly onto the mulch.

In an instant Emmy was back inside. Again she slammed the door, then burst into outraged tears.

"MOMMY!!" she shrieked. *"BONNIE'S LAUGHING AT ME!!"*

Chapter 4

GETTING IT ALL DONE

Marilyn Boyer is the best organized person I have ever met but she wasn't always that way. She has given me strict orders to make it clear that she is not an organizational genius and that she has learned the skills of orderliness a little at a time as the demand grew with the number people in our family. Several times moms have protested to her that they could never manage a large family and that she must be some kind of superlady. She wants to assure those moms that as God increases the responsibility, He increases the ability.

If it had been left up to me this chapter would never have been written. Marilyn is the brains of the outfit when it comes to making the household work smoothly. So the bulk of this chapter will be written using her notes for the lecture she gives on household organization for support groups and conventions. I make this disclaimer because I want her to get full credit for her contribution to the book. And because it would not be good for a reader to think I was the orderly one and end up inviting a guy who can't keep track of his own shoes to go somewhere and speak on household organization.

When we first came to Virginia as newlyweds it wasn't hard for Marilyn to keep our home organized. The advantage of having little in the way of worldly goods is that the built-in responsibility for caring for possessions is less when the possessions are few. Our two-bedroom mobile home came to us furnished and so we didn't lack for much except storage space. As I said, we didn't own a lot but what we had barely fit into that little box that was our home. Other than the limited space of our small cabinets and closets about the only optional storage we had was under our bed. I may be exaggerating but I seem to remember bumping my head on the ceiling if I sat up in bed carelessly.

Organize your space

We have found that the first thing that must be organized is the physical space of the home, including living space as well as storage. If that isn't orderly, it's very hard to organize your time, finances and possessions. This is something we're still learning about and I suspect we'll learn a lot more in the future because as Marilyn says, every time we do an organizational project she wonders why we didn't think of it years ago.

First, how do you identify your organizational needs? We've learned to use what we call an irritation list. This is a list of things that happen in the course of the day to irritate the lady of the house. When the list is made up it is then discussed at an appropriate time between husband and wife. Marilyn says this works best when it takes place over dinner in a restaurant. I can't explain that, but I'm not the organized one in the family. Anyway, in the course of the discussion you identify what type of need is causing the frustration. For example, it may be a physical need such as a lack of lighting. We had such a need in our combination storage room/workshop and added some florescent lights. Or the need may be behavioral and require some training sessions for the children. Once you have identified the cause of the irritation, you have to develop a project to meet the need.

Marilyn says that clutter is the enemy of orderliness. I have to admit if I was assigned to organize a room I'd rather it would be a room with nothing in it. So Marilyn is a great one for throwing things away and she is not oversensitive to

Yes, They're All Ours

whether the item in question is one of my treasured mementoes such as the rock I chiselled my name on in 1969. She says that throwing out should be made a family project that occurs at reasonable intervals to keep the buildup within limits. She also teaches the children the character quality of orderliness and what it means.

Once she feels that she has eliminated all unnecessary stuff (and a few things that I feel are necessary), then she tries to create an official place for every item that has recently appeared and so doesn't already have a place. Things are always out of place if they don't have a place. We can't keep our house organized without the help of the children, so we try not to discourage them by having more things in the house than place.

We've done a number of projects in the past to help with managing space. One project that I'm rather proud of is our shoe shelf. That's because I thought of it myself.

I built a shelf unit that looked like a bookcase. Nothing fancy, you understand, just something suitable for patching up and painting. Especially patching up. I took short pieces of the same lumber and made dividers on the shelves so that the whole thing is divided into compartments. Each compartment can hold two or three pairs of shoes under normal circumstances and more if you're not particular about being able to get them out again in a hurry. We fastened this thing to the wall in the down stairs entryway and loaded it down with about forty pairs of shoes, which left the closet floors then covered with only one layer of shoes, which we consider manageable.

Shoes are something to be reckoned with in our family. Imagine taking fourteen people on vacation and packing for each family member a pair of play shoes, a pair of dress shoes and a pair of shoes for all occasions in between. No wonder we don't take a lot of vacations.

46

Yes, They're All Ours

Another project was adding some bookshelves to my office, which also serves as the family library. We found that one bookcase can save a lot of floor space because a large one holds hundreds of books. We like tall bookcases.

Once we added dividers to the shelves in the bedroom closets. When you have at least two and sometimes three people sharing a closet this becomes necessary. We had tall stacks of sweaters, jeans, etc., which grew to a certain height and fell over. We put up with this for years before we finally saw a picture of a closet storage unit with dividers. We're sometimes a little slow on the uptake but that picture was all the inspiration we needed. The dividers have been a great help and now the stacks don't fall over until about the middle of December. That's when the search for hidden Christmas presents begins in earnest.

We don't have much of an attic because the roof of our house isn't very steep. You can't stand up in it but there was a lot of space going to waste up there until we bought some plywood and put a floor in. Then the only problem was the difficulty in getting Mom through the hatch in the ceiling to organize the boxes. We alternated for a long time between bringing in the stepladder for her and just hoisting a kid through the hatch with some stashing instructions. We had to floor the attic in stages because we never had the spare money to buy the plywood all at once. But little by little our storage space increased and the item that crowned it all was the pull-down stairwell we added as a separate project.

When we bought this house it hadn't been lived in for six months because it had been damaged by fire. We got it for a song of course but it was the blues that we ended up singing as we gradually encountered the many unseen expenses and difficulties of a major remodeling project. We got the mice and snakes cleared out in reasonably short order but oh, the junk. This was back in the days when the boys were too

47

small to help me a lot and I myself was past the tightening doorknobs point but not far. It was really dumb to take on a project like that but when you're dumb you aren't smart enough to know it, you see.

Anyway, there was a little hallway in the basement that wasn't needed so by a clever (for me) turn of carpentry I made it into a little storage room. It's hardly big enough to walk in but the walls are covered with shelves that hold extra bedding, craft supplies, game boxes, puzzles and so on. We also keep the vacuum in there somewhere. This little room has been a lesson in creating a tremendous amount of storage space in a little bit of floor space.

In the dining room which Marilyn also uses for a classroom, we added an additional bookshelf that holds not books but school supplies. That way pencils, paper, glue and all that stuff are all handy but out of the way.

Of course we still make use of that lovely space under the bed. It beats having to vacuum under there. Marilyn has a system of boxes and bags that I don't even comprehend and so I leave it alone. It's always interesting to see what new surprise will come forth into the light of day when my wife goes "shopping under the bed" as she calls it.

Do you have magazine holders in your house? We've found these to minimize clutter by containing the recent issues of several subscriptions. I'm not satisfied that there's not some better way, however. It seems to me that it's easy to neglect cycling out the older issues when the new ones arrive, resulting in some of the old ones staying too long, the holder getting crowded and magazines getting frazzled and torn up. For those issues we intend to save indefinitely we found cardboard boxes at the office supply store that hold ten or twenty magazines each and fit on the bottom shelf of a bookcase in my office with only the very top of the box squished.

Yes, They're All Ours

In our big storage room which is also the workshop, we found that we could make much better use of our shelf space by putting things in boxes and labeling the boxes. We also designated space on some the shelves for particular materials, automotive products for example. In that section we keep anti-freeze, wax, etc. We try to keep a case of motor oil on hand because we can buy it cheap at the auto supply store on sale. This is a necessity because we have five vehicles and there's always at least one leaking oil.

Organize your time

If you feel as if you're just beginning to get organized, so do we. But a little progress goes a long way toward motivating more progress. The main thing is to get started. Some women are sitting all day eating chocolates and watching soap operas because they've given up on making more productive use of their time. You'll find that organizing can be fun, but it isn't until you start. A good place to begin would be with an irritation list. Identify what you irritations are, take them one at a time and work them out. You'll feel encouraged immediately.

Marilyn suggests a spiral notebook with dividers for records. The sections will have to be changed all the time as the needs of the family change, but she finds that the flexibility of this method works better than the pre-packaged notebooks sold by the experts.

Some of her planning sections are:

Meals planning and grocery lists
"School " planning--books to order, science units, etc.
Kids' spiritual program--memory verses, character quality of the month, books to read, projects to do.
Mom's personal devotions--prayer and Scripture memory

49

Yes, They're All Ours

Daily Planning

My wife lives by lists because memory just isn't enough for her job. She makes lists of needed purchases, errands, appointments, bills to pay, and general to-do's. She even has a "things-to-do-when-I-get-time" list.

Organize your helpers

Marilyn says she couldn't survive if she didn't train her children to help with the work. She has daily and weekly schedules These schedules need to be like leather, strong but flexible. They have to flex with changing needs but be strong enough to hold together during times of stress and distraction.

The children have to be trained to perform the functions that the schedules call for. There is a security in knowing what is to be done at a certain time and how to do it. Marilyn assigns certain chores to certain children on certain days. Each day, the child knows what regular duties are his for the day. The chores on the daily chore list are to be done before 9:30 or 10 AM in time to start "school" work. Most of the chores rotate so that everybody gets a turn at the more and less pleasant chores. The exceptions are those jobs that are difficult enough that they require one of the older children, such as mowing the lawn.

In addition to the regular chores, there are some chores that we consider special effort and so we pay for them to be done. In addition to cash, we sometimes hand out different sorts of treats for special jobs such as washing the car or van. It's important, however not to pay for all chores. Children need to learn that the care of the family is partly the responsibility of each family member.

Yes, They're All Ours

The training of the children in chores is part of their training in character. They should be assigned chores that are within their abilities. You can't expect much of a two-year-old but a thirteen-year-old should be pulling his own weight. When the chores are assigned fairly, they should be performed properly. Work with the child through the job until he has the hang of it. Make sure he knows how to do the job right then hold him accountable to do it right. Give your children the tools for the work, too. They need the right tools for the right job and may get discouraged very easily if they don't have them.

Marilyn checks up on the kids and calls them back if the work isn't done properly. She has even been known to get a child out of bed to do a job over if it wasn't right the first time and it's a problem of irresponsibility rather than inability. But her discipline isn't all negative. From time to time she'll check a bedroom drawer and leave a candy bar in it if she finds it neat.

Even very young children can take a hand in the household work. Marilyn trains our two-year-olds to help with simple jobs such as drying the dishes and washing door facings. It would be much quicker to do the jobs herself than training the children to do them, but training pays off as years go by. Not only do the children know how to do the work, but they aren't afraid of work when they grow older and their ability and responsibility increase year by year.

The children get accustomed to doing their regular chores and don't have to be retrained every day. They also get used to non-regular chores such as the spring and fall cleaning. These "cleaning seasons" last for two or three weeks each and Marilyn writes a daily list of chores, adding one or two to each child's regular daily chores. Some examples are cleaning cobwebs, painting the fireplace, spot painting door trim and baseboards and window washing.

51

We believe that being regular members of the home maintenance staff is very good for children. It heads off slothfulness before it has a chance to take root, teaches children to accept responsibility, develops teamwork and makes everybody feel important. Everybody *is* important.

Discipline for order

The hardest person for me to discipline is myself. That's a sad fact but true in my case. I have learned that if I don't have myself under control I can't control the behavior of my children. If I throw temper tantrums, I can rest assured that they will too. If I'm an inconsistent father and pitch fits when something irritates me but punish my children for doing the same thing, they won't learn not to do it, but just not to do it in my presence. The Bible says that a man without control over his own spirit is as helpless as a city whose walls are broken down.

When we think of discipline, we usually think in terms of correction, of punishing misbehavior. But good discipline starts with demonstrating and then cultivating good behavior. Though we don't often think of it as such, a schedule is a great form of discipline. Not only does a schedule see that the important things get done, it also accustoms us to doing things based on a set requirement rather than on what we do or don't feel like doing. If you are home educator for instance, and you have your textbook work scheduled for the same time of day five days a week, there won't be this business of "Oh, Mom, do we have to do 'school' today?" because we do it every day. It's as much habit as eating at regular hours.

We'll say more about child discipline later. For now we want to emphasize a few basic points about "getting it all done" in a house full of people.

Yes, They're All Ours

You must organize or you will agonize. If you waste your time you will waste your life because life is made of time. Start with the most common irritations in your life and use them as keys to where to start organizing. Organize your surroundings, your materials, your time and your helpers.

We still have our "zoo days" at the House of Boyer. That's a part of being a family. But I shudder to think what would happen if my second in command hadn't learned over the years to put her house in order.

A word to the home educators

Because we have met so many parents in our home education work who feel a need for a lot more orderliness in their ministry to their children, we wanted to address some thoughts to their specific situation as home educators.

Identify God's priorities for your time

Streamline your schedule. If you want to get the most important things in life done, then you will have to stay away from some other things that are good expenditures of time, but not the best. When you have a large family you don't have as much time for outside activities as other people do. One thing you will learn if you haven't already is that time is like money in that it always seems to be in short supply and there are plenty of people who are eager to help you spend it.

It is critically important to learn how to say no because there so many good opportunities that they are constantly trying -to crowd out the best. If you are the type of person who likes to help others, meet needs and make productive use of your time you will be in great demand. In the short time since my son was elected chairman of our political party's county organization I've been amazed at how many people are calling to enlist him in some cause. He now has some influence because of his position and the work he did to get elected to that position demonstrated to others that he is diligent and motivated.

Churches are among the guilty parties who tempt moms to be over-committed at the cost of their families. Most churches have too many programs and are always looking for leaders and helpers. Unfortunately, most of the folks from church who call you up looking for help are not in a position to know what your other commitments are (nobody knows the trouble I's seen) and so may use a little more persuasion than they would if they understood. If you're going to keep your priorities straight, you'll have to develop some sensitivity to the Lord and discern which opportunities you can afford and which you can't..

The evaluation and sifting of available activities is a process that is ongoing. You won't be able to set a weekly schedule and follow it strictly forever because your responsibilities will change from month to month and year to year.

You'll find you need to streamline your children's schedule too. I've heard of moms who try to get a little bookwork done in the car because of all the time they spent in transit. They had their children overcommitted to activities which were supposedly educational and yet they were spending more time traveling between activities than they did at anything else. A little yellow sign in the back window designating the vehicle as 'Mom's Taxi' is the equivalent of a white flag. It proclaims Mom's surrender to the forces that are pressuring her to have her children in so many extracurricular activities that there is no time for curricular activities. Don't forget that home education requires some time at home.

Yes, They're All Ours

There are more activities available to children than there are to adults in the Christian community. Many parents assume that since all of them seem to have some value, the child will benefit the most by being involved in the most activities possible. 'Tain't so. Home is where the best learning happens. The Boyers stay home a lot. In our town we have dozens of activities available for our children, most of which would be considered to have some educational value. But we believe that for basic education it's hard to find a better arrangement than a mom, a child and a pile of good books. Doesn't that simplicity sound appealing after some of the ordeals of activities you've been through?

Remember that the most important activity of all is spiritual activity. We tend to do to our children what we do to ourselves-- get loaded down with time commitments and let spiritual things slide. Don't be guilty of being on time for Little League practice but putting spiritual training time off until another day.

If you don't design your schedule to demand time for Scripture memorization, Bible reading, concordance study (for the older children), spiritual training projects, reading Bible stories, etc., it won't get done. These things must be scheduled in as priorities or the multitudes of options will crowd them out.

Speaking of streamlining, you'll need to streamline your child's curriculum as well as his schedule. Just because instructions are in the book doesn't mean they're all essential. You must check out the requirements of the curriculum material your child uses and determine what is worth his time and what isn't. Some of the requirements of textbooks are just busywork.

For instance, we don't assign lists of spelling words for most of our children. All our children are good readers and good readers are usually good spellers. I'm an exxelunt spelar myself. For the one or two of our children who needed practice specifically in spelling, we have found that usually the problem is a violation of one or two of the spelling rules. So we give them lists of words that reflect those rules (for example, 'receive' for the rule about i before e except after c etc.) and review the rules they seem to have a problem with. This is a far cry from having all the children bore themselves to tears working through all the word lists in the spellers representing all the rules, including the ones nobody is having trouble with. As home educators one of the ways in which we mimic schools (and reduce our effectiveness) is to make assignments for all in response to the needs of a few.

We wait until around fourth grade level before teaching spelling and third grade level for language. This is radically different from most schools but we have found that children will correct so many of their own mistakes with the passage of time that it's inefficient to add a lot of drudgery to the early years. Then whatever weaknesses remain can be identified, isolated and dealt with.

Especially in the case of younger children, let them answer questions orally when there is no need for a written response, which there seldom is. Children can't write nearly as fast as they talk, and can't talk nearly as fast as they think. When they're required to slow down their thinking to the speed of their writing it can be very frustrating. Schools are forever labeling children LD (Learning Disabled) and ADD (Attention Deficit Disorder) when it's the school that has the problem. If I had to sit in a desk for hours and answer a lot of questions in writing that I could answer orally in a fraction of the time I'd get bored too. No telling what label they'd hang on me.

Of course children need to learn neat handwriting. But for the younger children sessions need to be kept short and tied to a useful purpose such as writing a letter to Grandma.

Yes, They're All Ours

Writing for the sake of practicing writing is surely one of the most demotivating exercises ever created.

All this talk about streamlining your curriculum boils down to the simple goal of giving your child the best learning possible while making the best use of your time. Besides tailoring your structured curriculum to the needs of your own family, there are a number of things you can do to enhance learning and without a lot of time expended, too.

Because of the time demands in our household, we've looked for creative ways to encourage learning outside the structure of the text materials (call it extracurricular if you must). The idea is to enrich your home environment to make it more fertile for learning to grow in. You have done the same thing with your garden. When we moved to our present home we found that we had very poor soil so we enriched it with several loads of a fragrant substance we obtained at the local livestock market. Fortunately, it will not be necessary to shovel cattle compost all over your living room floor. We're talking about growing learning, not tomatoes.

There are all kinds of valuable learning tools for your home which will cost no more than useless toys and furnishings. There are lots of educational toys available if you'll put out a little effort instead of just grabbing a (God forbid) Barbie doll off the shelf to save the time expense of making decisions. Marilyn found a color-coded wall clock to teach the children to tell time. Our kids used to play with a plastic inflatable kick ball that was a globe. We found some sheets for Boom's bed with the geography of the world on them. He used to get his younger sisters on his top bunk and teach them the continents.

Have plenty of books in the house, but only good ones. When you find a new book that you'd like to see your children read, introduce it to them or just 'plant' it on somebody's bed or the coffee table. There are plenty of other good publications too. I've told you about Rickey's political magazines, which not only satisfy his interest but pique the curiosity of the other children just by lying around the house. There are a wide range of magazines dealing with science, history, art, and so forth as well.

Some of the best reading for children and adults alike is in the form of biographies of good people, especially great Christians. Scripture indicates that we become like the people with whom we keep company. Our experience bears this out, too, so we try to provide good company for our children in the form of books about people whose lives are exemplary. The *Childhood of Famous Americans* series, available at public libraries and through a number of book catalogs, is excellent. You have to be careful though, because some of their newer books are about people you would not offer as heroes to your children, for example John L. Lewis the union organizer. On the other hand, they have the old standbys such as Washington, Lincoln, Edison, Carver and the others. Another good series is the *Sower Series*, a set of Christian biographies for older children.

The older your children get, the more they need godly role models. As they grow up and discover that there are other adults in the world besides Mom and Dad, they begin to look around and notice the lives of people outside the family and evaluate their attitudes and values. Through the medium of Christian biographies they can have exposure to people whose influence on them will be strong and positive.

Both for learning and recreation, it's good to have a supply of art supplies on hand. Our younger children especially spend a lot of time at the craft area in our basement. Marilyn has collected popsicle sticks, a glue gun, paints, clay, etc., and these things make a much healthier pastime than being babysat by a television. It's surprising how much time children can spend happily putting a new paint job on a toy car.

While we're on the subject of time management, don't forget the negative side of the question. There are a million things that can butt into your family life and waste valuable time or even do damage. In our day as never before, discernment is needed not only to fill the home with good things, but to eliminate the harmful influences as well.

Television is one of my favorite whipping boys because so many people fall victim to it, it did so much damage to me as a child and the evidence against it is so clear. Also, it's so addictive. Whenever I talk about the dangers of television I get strikingly strong reactions from some people, even in the home education community where people are more sensitive to such things. But I've never heard anyone defend television who is not addicted to it. Parents can get addicted to television without even watching it by growing dependent on it as a babysitter. The Plug-in Drug, as it's called in the title of the superb book by Marie Winn, can grab a child's attention and hold it for hours. It seems to be awfully easy for moms to grow addicted to the convenience ease of quieting the children by hitting a button on a remote control gizmo.

There is a lot more to say on the subject of TV but I've already said a lot in my book The Socialization Trap so I won't duplicate the effort here. Certainly wouldn't want to discourage you from buying another book.

While we're on the subject of electronic distractions, though, let me offer a word of caution about VCR's. Those things are being more and more widely used by Christian parents who object to television but still like the convenience of the babysitting feature. I can only see allowing a VCR in your home if it is used strictly for educational purposes. They can be useful but oh, the temptation to use them for entertainment. There are lots of videos on the market that would seem to be harmless, such as the old Disney movies (before they became so saturated with New Age occultism). But these still are powerful time wasters and serve to fill the mind with false philosophies and values. Marilyn and I once watched Disney's version of *Swiss Family Robinson* at the home of friends and found it disgusting. The movie was made back in the early sixties or even earlier, but it was junk. If you've ever read the book by Johann Wyss you'll find the video a pale caricature with the frequent family prayers of the Robinsons reduced to practically none and Papa Robinson's godly exhortations replaced by shallow conversation. We cheated ourselves by spending the time on it. But if movies made thirty years ago were empty, how would you describe the modern ones? The old ones were vanity and folly. The new ones (for the most part) are poisoned with godlessness, sensuality and occultism.

At the risk of seeming extreme, I have to say that I don't believe a child can reach his full potential in a home in which television or VCR's are used for entertainment. Totally aside from any immorality in the programming, electronic entertainment soaks up time that would be better used in almost any other diversion, detracts from family relationships, limits communication, distracts from responsibilities and absorbs energy that should be invested in healthy play and learning. Most video kids are not avid readers and tree climbing is better for the muscles.

Reading material, like entertainments, needs to be screened carefully. You wouldn't let your child eat food from a dumpster because you know that such food, though it might contain some nutritional elements, is likely to be contaminated with harmful germs. So it is with reading material.

Yes, They're All Ours

One day Marilyn and I ran into a lady friend in a store. As we chatted with her for a minute I noticed that her son was standing by a rack of comic books and reading one. Our friend commented on what an appetite her son had for reading and how glad she was that he was so literate. She seemed to have no objection to his reading comic books, though I'm aware that most of them contain generous doses of occultism and little that would seem very healthy. We seem to have the idea that any reading material is good but this is far from the truth. Reading is the interpreting of writing, writing is the recording of words, words are the expression of thoughts and thoughts are the building blocks of attitudes and values. When we read we are exposed to the values of the writer and his characters and a certain amount of their philosophy is going to rub off on the subconscious mind. We need to think through where our children are getting their thoughts. What values does Spider Man have?

We are very conservative about what our children read, but there is plenty of good reading material in the world. Besides biographies there is are nature books, how-to-do-it type books, history and so on. We severely limit fiction, and more so in the early years. We don't have much use for fiction at all and particularly fantasy, although we like some historical fiction. After all, *Pilgrim's Progress* is fiction.

Another aspect of the counterproductivity issue is that of companionship. Our children are playmates for each other and it's a good thing it's that way because there are few others with whom we want our children spending their time. Scripture says that he who walks with wise men shall be wise and the companion of fools shall suffer harm. It also specifically tells us not to hang around with certain character types, including immoral persons, angry persons, thieves, drunkards and gluttons. There have been an awful lot of young lives damaged by keeping company with the wrong crowd so we're very protective of our children. Even if we only had one or two children and some might think they lacked social contact, we are more interested   in quality of companionship than quantity.

We don't allow our kids to just "go play" at another chlid's home because we have no control over what goes on in that home. We've pretty well trained the neighbor children to ask permission before dropping over to play at our house and we don't allow the children's friends to play here when neither Marilyn or I are at home. We often say no to little visitors much as we hate to, because we just don't like the influence of so much that we see in the lives of their families.

We think the ideal relationship to have with neighbors is one of ministry. We certainly need to do more of this, but we have had some good experiences in the past. Once our children put on a neighborhood party and used it as an opportunity to tell the other children about Jesus while feeding them hot dogs and chips.

If by now you've forgotten that we're talking about getting things done, perhaps I've drifted too far off course. But we need to be reminded that we will never accomplish God's goals--that is, "getting it all done" from His point of view--if we don't chart a course based on the most worthy goals and give it all we've got. We need to learn to say no to the cheap and unworthy enticements of this world whether in entertainment, companionship or simple self-indulgence.

FAMILY SNAPSHOTS
Part IV

Sometimes there are good laughs in the way children interpret what adults say.

Josh, age three, was standing on the high chair watching Mom working at the sink. In his clumsy, nasal speech he kept nagging her to hurry up and finish with her chore so that she could get him a treat she had just promised.

"Huwwy up, Mommy," he begged.

"Now, Joshie, just hold your horses a minute."

The little boy looked around him, wide eyed and confused.

"Wheah ah they?"

We get our cars serviced at a garage owned by a member of our church, Cecil Staton. One day Marilyn was on her way out the door to deliver the latest patient. Seeing Mommy about to leave, two-year-old Gracie wanted to know as always where she was headed.

"I'm taking the van to Mr. Staton," Mommy explained.

Little Gracie's eyes grew big and she looked frightened.

"No! Not *Satan*!" she exclaimed.

We've been taking our cars to "Mr. Cecil" ever since.

Chapter 5

HOW CAN YOU AFFORD IT?

"Do you have a million dollars, Daddy?" Bill asked.
"No," said Dad a little ruefully. "I have a million children, instead. Somewhere along the line, a man has to choose between the two."

from *Cheaper by the Dozen*

If you have children it will come as no surprise to you that I'm occasionally asked how I manage to feed twelve of them. I confess it's a question I have posed to myself from time to time. As you can imagine, a month's groceries for a family of fourteen carries approximately the same price tag as a nose job for Jimmy Durante.

We go through seven gallons of milk in a week and we could double that if we let the children drink all they want. When the boys and I were taking sandwiches all the time for our lunches at work we were using twenty loaves of bread a week. Marilyn buys boxes of paper towels, thirty-six rolls per box. Soap comes in packages of twelve bars, which last for two weeks. We can use seven pounds of potatoes in one meal and a large cake disappears for dessert. We don't eat a lot of unusual stuff, just unusual amounts. Marilyn typically doubles or triples recipes. She had to give up on cereal for breakfast and now serves muffins and such instead. Two boxes of cereal per day was getting expensive.

My wife buys cheese in five-pound blocks. Large boxes of crackers are gone as soon as they're opened. Marilyn found a place to buy laundry detergent in fifty-pound buckets. She uses a bucket in three weeks.

The family owns a truck and a van for use in the drywall business in addition to Rick's station wagon which Mom

64

sometimes drives and so which we help to maintain. When we travel as a group we drive the family fifteen-passenger van. By the way, Rick has a work van, too. All this keeps Staton & Sons auto service busy and our home looking like a used car lot. You can imagine the expense.

I've been in the trenches too long to see the topic of finances through rose colored glasses. Meaning no disrespect, I'm hard to impress with the testimony of some eighteen-year-old college student in a choral group who received twenty dollars in answer to prayer when the handwriting on the envelope looked more like that of his rich aunt than any that was ever found on tablets of stone on Mt. Sinai.

Don't get me wrong now. George Muller is one of my all-time heroes of the faith and I firmly believe in God's ability and His willingness to supply the needs of His children. I believe that He has many times provided even supernaturally, as He did for Elijah through the instrumentality of a group of ravens with some strange behavior patterns. But not everybody is called to walk the same path as Mr. Muller, as he himself said. The usual way that God provides man's needs is by the sweat of his brow. He that will not work, neither shall he eat.

In the very early days of my married life (which was the first time I had faced the responsibility of providing for anyone other than myself) I was delighted to read and hear about a number of instances in which God had miraculously supplied material needs through prayer. I heard some preaching that suited me very well on the subject of giving and receiving. Just sow bountifully, they said. He that soweth bountifully shall reap also bountifully. Thirty, sixty, even a hundredfold. Yea, verily.

So I tried some seed giving to see if I could prime the celestial pump. Not that my motives were entirely selfish, you understand. It's just that the line between faith and speculation was a little bit fuzzy.

I didn't wait long for the arrival of ravens (hopefully with beakfuls of fifty-dollar bills) before I backed off and decided there must be a little more to this faith business than meets the eye. My education in financial freedom had just begun and is still continuing to this day as I seem to have a certain degree of LD in the subject. Many, varied and memorable have been the lessons in my course of study. And a veritable fountain of pleasures it has been, I assure you.

I want to review my business career in some detail because I'm satisfied that I started out more ignorant than the vast majority of my readers and have now reached the point where I own a modest family business that reasonably meets the needs of one whopper of a family. I hope that will be encouraging to those who read this and may be now where I was twenty years ago. If, God forbid, any of them are.

I grew up about as ignorant of financial matters as a person can be. I never held a job growing up except for some very brief stints at odds and ends of work of quite menial types. When I was a small boy, My dad would occasionally make me go to work with him, which was torture to me. Not only was I too little to do much of the actual work, which would have made it more interesting, but he was a house painter. His work couldn't have interested me if I'd been allowed to run the whole business.

I used to complain as much as I dared and whiningly ask Dad why I had to do something as unpleasant as going to work. He'd always have the same deep, philosophical answer.

"Because you need to learn how to make a living."

See what I mean? You couldn't reason with the man.

I didn't dare say much because Dad's fuse wasn't terribly long. But I knew just how it was. When I finally turned

eighteen and got paroled from school, I was going to go back
to the Ozarks and build myself a log cabin and be a farmer.
Just how I was going to pay for the land was a detail I never
got around to resolving. Anyway, I was going to fish and
hunt and plow the fields with my big brown horses (which I
guess were going to just magically appear out of nothingness
like the farm). But even if I had been open to the idea of a
regular job, one thing I would never, never, never, never,
ever under any circumstances even for a second give a
molecule of consideration to doing was something as
horrible and boring as painting houses.

Would you care to guess how I ended up spending five
long years? Psalm 2 says that the Lord sits in the heavens
and laughs. Dad is up there now so the Lord isn't laughing
alone.

I've confessed before that I arrived in Lynchburg in 1974
as a twenty-two-year-old with a wife, a month-old son, a car
payment, two large dogs and twenty-eight dollars in my
pocket. Sam Walton I was not. This situation was typical of
what my wife's parents had feared would happen. In the
days when we were talking about getting married they had
warned us that we needed some financial preparation. They
had grown up during the Depression and after Marilyn's dad
came home from World War II he had built a business by
sweat and will power. They took economics very seriously
and were concerned about their daughter's future. In my
twenty-year-old omniscience I had assured them that the
Lord would always provide. My Unitarian future parents-in-
law were not greatly relieved.

To spare Marilyn some painful memories I will pass over
some of the contortions we went through until permanent
living arrangements could be made. We shall fast forward
instead to a few weeks after our arrival.

Yes, They're All Ours

With the aid of a gift from my grandmother we had put a down payment on a mobile home and had moved in. In mid-January I started school and was all geared up to become a hotshot young youth pastor. We were living on a few hundred dollars a month from the G.I. Bill, supplemented by whatever I could earn in my off hours.

I applied to a local detective agency and got some part-time work as a security guard. Through the college employment office I picked up some odd jobs cutting grass and so forth, and some work came in through word of mouth contacts as well. Still, there never seemed to be quite enough to make ends meet. The constant financial pressure strained our relationship and constantly distracted me from my educational efforts. I was supposed to be there to get smart but it was impossible to concentrate on homework with all the stress. My grades were as low as my spirits.

One evening Marilyn and I were going over (and over and over) our budget, getting more and more depressed. Finally I burst out in frustration, "What it actually means is that we just can't afford to live!" Then another thought struck me. "But come to think of it, we can't afford to die, either." We didn't have cemetery lots or burial insurance.

This was not at all the way it was supposed to work. I had come to this town to be trained in the work of the Lord. He was supposed to meet my financial needs, supernaturally if necessary, and my faith was supposed to grow stronger continually. Somebody had fallen down on the job and I was sure it wasn't me. After all, there were other young couples in school, lots of them. Some of them even lived in our trailer park. And their needs were being met, weren't they?

Actually, I suspect that we were all starving but everybody thought they were the only ones and felt unspiritual admitting it.

Yes, They're All Ours

Another thing that didn't add up was the whole mentality palmed off as spirituality on the married students. One older man who was a student there verbalized the prevailing philosophy for me with conviction.

"The way to do it, Rick, is go to class in the morning, go to work in the afternoon, walk in the house in the evening, say, 'Marilyn, see ya later' and go into the bedroom to hit the books until bed time."

The fact that he was living on a military retirement pension might have had something to do with his casual attitude. Not having to work a job, he had nothing to do but go to class and do homework. Marilyn, however, was not at all impressed with that viewpoint and I wasn't crazy about it either. We hadn't gotten married because we liked being strangers. Yet, we were intimidated by the conventional wisdom that all this conflict between education and family life was just a normal part of the commendable sacrifice we were making for the Lord. The thing to do, it was assumed, was to study hard, work a job, be involved in all the church and school activities to get experience, and never be home with your wife. Which didn't matter anyway, because she was supposed to be out working a job of her own to help with school expenses.

A Sunday school class changed our direction forever. The Family Focus class was comprised mostly of young couples and somebody suggested it to us almost as soon as we moved to Lynchburg. The class was taught by Larry Coy, a man who had worked with Institute in Basic Life Principles in their early days. That great ministry was to have a profound effect on our family later, but our first exposure to the Biblical principles that would change our lives came in Larry Coy's Sunday school class.

Here we heard some things that lifted tremendous burdens for us. We were taught that God wants a man's first priority

69

to be his relationship with the Lord, his second his wife, and then his children. Career and ministry (beyond his ministry to his family) came later.

Another milestone had been reached. You can imagine Marilyn eating all this up and it was just as much relief to me. There remained a problem, though. The teaching we were receiving in Sunday school was contradicted constantly by the philosophy of the college I was attending. On the one hand I was being told to make my family number one after the Lord Himself, and on the other hand that neglecting my family was a sacrifice for the Lord. It was an uncomfortable several months as we tried to work through all this.

One day we heard in Sunday school about an Old Testament law that provided for stability in the first year of marriage. It comes from Deuteronomy 24:5:

When a man hath taken a new wife, he shall not go out to war, neither shall he be charged with any business: *but* he shall be free at home one year, and shall cheer up his wife which he hath taken.

From a simple reading of this verse it's clear that a man in Old Testament Israel was not to serve in the military during his first year of marriage. But what was the meaning of the reference to being "charged" with any "business?" On looking up the Hebrew words in the text I got the impression that the English translation was pretty accurate. The intent seemed to be that no responsibilities were to be required of the newly married man other than those attendant to marriage. The man who was substitute teaching for Larry the Sunday this came up believed that the newlywed was not even to work a job, but to take a year off from business entirely and concentrate on making his wife happy. I never studied the matter in enough depth to satisfy myself as to the correctness of his opinion because I never had any such option. But I commented to my wife that a year-long honeymoon sounded good to me. She replied that it did only if it wasn't a replay of the honeymoon we'd already had. Some people.

After class I went up to the teacher with a question.

"I'm in college here. I've been married for almost two years and I sure didn't have a first year like you described. What would you think of the idea of taking a year off starting now?"

"I think it'd be great, if you can afford it."

"No, I don't mean off work, I could never afford that. I mean a year off from school."

The guy was very encouraging and I didn't need a whole lot of prodding. Marilyn and I discussed it and agreed quickly. It was like having a mountain lifted off our shoulders.

I think I was still taking summer classes at the time. At any rate I was very soon looking for a full-time job and I didn't re-enter college in the fall. I took some flak from well-meaning people associated with the school including some fellow students. But I was happy to believe that I was being more spiritual by taking a year off from Bible college to concentrate on my family. I assured everybody that I'd be back in a year.

I wasn't. In October of that year I landed a job as a tracking dog handler for the Virginia prison system and as I said before, that was the entry into the real world for me. I had already said farewell to the enforced security and structure of military life and now I bade a fond adieu to Bible college. I never did become a youth pastor. But as I would gradually come to understand, there was an education waiting for me that I could not have gotten from school and a ministry ahead which was very different and very much more important than the one I had envisioned

It was with a heady sense of my own importance that I entered upon my first real job. I was now twenty-three years old, eager, audacious and sure that I was headed for great things.

The prison system was definitely educational. My life had been sheltered in some ways before that. I had grown up in a midwestern small-town atmosphere where the high school was still drug free. Now I was working among men who had been confined together for the sole reason that they were bad. I found that when criminals are dumped together to simmer in their own juices they just get worse. In fact the idea of confinement as punishment is an unscriptural concept. It fails to provide for restitution to the victim and provides instead for a place where small-time offenders are thrown in with old pro crooks who can teach the amateurs more effective ways to do wrong. Prisons are a breeding ground for vice and perversion. A return to Biblical principles such as restitution, corporal punishment and swift and certain execution for crimes designated as capital offenses would do this nation a world of good. It would also do individuals much good because it would dissuade many more people from entering into a multitude of sins.

In the prison system I learned a lot about people. The inmates had little to do to amuse themselves except watch television and scheme up ways to gain some miniscule advantage for themselves or do some harm to someone else, which was considered just as satisfactory. With some exceptions, the favorite target of any mischief was a prison employee. We represented the authority they hated and many of them lost no opportunity to do any little thing that would irritate a guard.

Yes, They're All Ours

If your concept of prison life comes from the old convict movies featuring men in stripes, vicious Bloodhounds baying on the trail and sadistic guards who beat and kick prisoners for recreation, you've never worked in a modern prison. In Virginia at least, stripes went out decades ago. Bloodhounds are gentle, mild-tempered dogs who very seldom exhibit aggressiveness. And by the way they don't bay on the trail, either. If they ever did it was bred out of them long ago by sensible men who didn't want their whereabouts broadcast to the possibly dangerous people they were chasing. As for the brutality of guards to prisoners, it's usually the other way around. If a prisoner ever gets hurt or killed, it's nearly always by another inmate. The ACLU has seen to it that the handcuffs are on the good guys and the criminals are handled with kid gloves.

That was one of my two main complaints while I worked for the prison system. The other was that inmates didn't escape often enough. As I said, I was then bold, eager and fifty pounds lighter and I absolutely loved pursuing a criminal through the woods with a good dog ahead of me and a .38 on my hip. John Wayne, no less.

My job was to travel around the state to medium-security institutions called road camps and help the officers in charge of the tracking dogs there with the training of the hounds. Then whenever there was an escape anywhere in Virginia I could be called upon to throw a dog from my home camp in the back of my personally customized dog truck and roar off down the highway with a cloud of dust and a hearty 'Hi-yo Silver!' I was very hot stuff.

It's funny how that sort of thing gets into one's blood. I heard the jingle of the telephone in the middle of the night so often that I developed record-breaking speed in dressing and getting to camp. It didn't matter how late I had gotten to bed or how much I had moaned and groaned to Marilyn at

73

bedtime how exhausted I was. When that 2 AM call came I was out of bed, down the hall and had the receiver in my hand by halfway through the second ringie-dingie. In a heartbeat the guy who had not a molecule of energy left at day's end was jerking on his clothes and strapping on his pistol with a "Yippee, we got a manhunt! I'm outa here!" My wife will testify that it was years before I stopped going ballistic at the ring of a midnight phone call.

Looking back almost twenty years it seems that my career in the prison system lasted a long time but in fact it was only about a year. I guess the reason I have so many memories I've hung onto is that it was the first and last interesting job I ever had. How strange is the makeup of a young man's heart that even when he's pretty well off he can find so many little things with which to be discontent and forever be throwing himself out of the frying pan into the fire.

It was again finances that occasioned a change of course for me. Marilyn was home with our then two little boys as she should be and we were living on my state paycheck alone. We were making ends meet but just barely. We hardly ever ate out and I seldom even bought myself a Coke in my travels for the state. I received a cost-of-living increase each year, but my outgo was still growing faster than my income and I began to look for options.

Leaving college was a good move and leaving my dog job was a bad one. What the two decisions had in common was that both were aided and abetted by my tendency to follow advice, particularly if it was the kind I wanted to hear.

I felt that there was no future for me in the prison system. Pay raises in my own job were too slow to keep up with the needs of my growing family and the only way to move up in the system it appeared, was to give up my beloved hounds and go to work as a regular guard then work my way up to sergeant. I knew enough about the torturous boredom that is the lot of the average prison guard to know that I could never stand it. On the few occasions I had allowed myself to be suckered into standing in for an 'inside' officer for an hour or two I had felt like a prisoner myself. I went crazy. I wasn't long on creative alternatives at that age and besides as I said I was always discontent and hungry for change. So when I received some very bad advice that happened to suit my tastes I followed it. I regretted it soon after and I still do.

Just as it's easy to follow advice that tells you to do something you think you'd like to do, it's also tempting to advise others to do things you'd like to do but can't. I fell victim to both syndromes when I decided to leave the prison system. I had spoken about my problem with a man who had done a lot of Christian counseling. He advised me to do as a friend of his had done. Joe had started his own business and made big money. I liked both ideas.

I later came to suspect that my advisor would like to have had Joe's money himself and that he hoped to enjoy some vicarious success in watching me build a big business. I don't know if he ever got rich but there's no doubt I disappointed him.

When I had gone to talk to him he had told me all about Joe. Joe had worked in a factory and wanted some extra income. So he went knocking on doors asking how he could be of service. He would be happy to do anything around the house, he said. He didn't know how to do anything, but when somebody hired him for a job he'd call up a friend who had the requisite skills and ask a few questions, then jump in. He botched some jobs but was willing to do them over until he got them right. By the time Joe got laid off from his factory job a few years later he had built up a clientele in his side business and he just gracefully slid into doing that full-time. After one short year he had had to buy a second truck and hire a helper. And everybody lived happily ever after.

I listened to the story with increasing eagerness. I could be my own boss. I could make good money. I could pull myself up by the bootstraps. I was going to start out with nothing and go to the top. I'd make Horatio Alger proud.

So give me a break. I was only a kid.

Never one to jump into things suddenly I took a couple of days vacation time from my dog job and went knocking on doors. No sense taking a leap without a season of preparation. I found several people who wanted things done. My excitement grew as I began to see for myself the potential of self-employment. When I went back to work on Monday I turned in my notice.

Of course my new home maintenance business was a disaster immediately. Every job I did took longer than expected and sometimes I couldn't get it done right no matter how hard I tried. Going back to my counselor friend for advice I was told, "Hey man, ya gotta learn." My wife, who always greets me in the evening by asking how my day was, grew accustomed to the same answer repeated often: "Well, I didn't make any money but I sure learned a lot." She got to the point where she didn't ask for many of the details.

I had entered the world of self-employment under just about every unfavorable condition possible except a major economic depression, and soon I had one of those going too. If you don't remember the Great Depression of the mid-1970's it's because I kept it to myself.

While I was marching off in bold conquest, confident of victory, a man with more life experience would have foreseen disaster. I had started a home maintenance business knowing nothing of home maintenance and nothing of business. I had no money, no contacts, no truck, no tools, no clientele, no insurance, no skills. Especially no skills.

You'll understand my ill-preparedness for a home maintenance career when I tell you about my doorknobs.

76

Yes, They're All Ours

During my year in the prison system we had bought our first house and said farewell to our crackerbox mobile home. The new house was very small but comfortable for us and everything in it was brand new. For a long time we didn't have any trouble with anything in it except the doorknobs. Those things started getting loose when we had only been in the house for a few weeks. As time went by they got looser and looser until most of them rattled and the one in our bedroom pulled halfway out of the hole in the door when we tried to use it.

I was indignant. We had bought a brand new house and the doorknobs were coming off. The jerks who built the house didn't even know enough to buy doorknobs that wouldn't fall apart. What was wrong with people? I would wax eloquent when the mood was on me and I found loose doorknobs particularly irritating. I could start with doorknobs and launch into an exposition on all that was wrong with American industry and craftsmanship from doorknobs to General Motors. One thing that was a long time in occurring to me though, was the possibility that I could fix the doorknobs myself. Rick Boyer couldn't fix anything.

One day I paused for a moment in grasping a rattly handful of doorknob as I was about to walk out of the bedroom and did something I hadn't thought to do before. I looked at it. That's right, I looked at it. In fact I bent over a little and gave it a careful appraisal just on the off chance that I might be able to see what the problem was. I couldn't identify anything clearly wrong; I had never really looked at a doorknob before. But I did notice the heads of two screws protruding through holes in the round metal plate between the door and the knob. I thought, "Now I wonder what would happen if I turned those screws?"

Yes, They're All Ours

The screws had little X-shaped slots in them in which a screwdriver was supposed to fit. I knew I had a screwdriver with a point like that so I went to get it and began to turn those screws. In the right direction. On the very first try. And would you believe it, the gap between the door and the knob just magically began to shrink. I kept turning those screws and watching the doorknob move while a feeling of inspiration welled up inside me. In no time at all the thing was snug on the door and I couln't have rattled it if I'd tried. I stood staring in awe at the screwdriver in my hand. Revelation.

I guess I was pretty naive in failing to see that I wasn't the ideal candidate for a home maintenance business. But my counselor had been so upbeat about it all. It was too bad he didn't emphasize the fact that when Joe started his business he had several years' worth of part-time experience under his belt. Home maintenance might have been a very good sideline for me, supplementing my income and providing me with opportunities to learn a variety of handy skills. But to go into it as I did with no preparation and depending on it for my entire income was just plain stupid.

Another reason the affair was a mess was that I am not a thing person and home maintenance is all about things. When I say a thing person I mean a person who is inclined toward working with physical materials as opposed to working with people or ideas. I know now that I am a people person. I love speaking to groups or with a single individual. I would have been quite suitable to teaching or sales or counseling. My mother always said I should be a lawyer because I could talk my way out of anything. But when it came to working with my hands I was out of my element, as my doorknobs demonstrated.

Now here I was, twenty-four years old and facing the consequences of a huge blunder. A family to feed and wanting to be responsible but totally unsuitable to the type of work to which I had committed myself. A mule won't win the Kentucky Derby not matter how good his intentions are.

If people in Heaven pay much attention to what goes on down here, Dad was starting to grin about this time and soon he would be laughing out loud. Because as I knocked on hundreds of doors asking for work I heard one word repeated over and over. Painting. People seem to love to love the smell of paint because it seemed everybody in Lynchburg, Virginia wanted some painting done. For the first few months in the life of my new business I had plenty of work. And truthfully, I didn't mind the painting so much at first. The reason I came to hate painting was the very reason I had so much painting to do: I didn't know how to estimate the work and so I consistently gave bids that were too low. It seemed folks were delighted to meet me.

In addition to bidding too cheaply, I was an inexperienced painter and took much longer to do the work than an old pro would have taken. After a few months of doing work that I didn't really care for at prices that guaranteed starvation, my attitude began to suffer as much as my income. If you're going to succeed at an enterprise, it needs to be something for which you are suited and for which you have some motivation. If you continually fail, you lose your motivation. If you lose your motivation you will continually fail. It's a vicious cycle that's hard to break.

By the time I gave up Miracle Maintenance (you may blame old Joe for that hokey name, because like some other bad ideas I borrowed it from him) I was ten months older and felt as if it were ten years. I took a job in restaurant management which was more in my line being people work, but other job pressures drove me out after six months. I took some painting contracts and even cut and sold firewood for a while. The following spring I went back to school hoping to reenter law enforcement work, supported by some painting jobs and the G. I. Bill. After a few months of school I was hired as deputy sheriff and thought I was finally making progress toward an interesting career. But the job paid less than the job I had left in the prison system two years before and I gave it up after six months. Now I found myself back in the horrible painting business and somewhere up there Dad was laughing his head off.

If you've never had a job you hated but couldn't quit, you may have a hard time empathizing with me. Painting, after all, is not as bad as some things. Say, being horsewhipped or adrift at sea for a year in a rubber raft. But I can assure you I hated it. I hated it so much in fact that I hated life.

It was desperately hard to get out of bed in the morning and drag myself out the door for what I knew would be a miserable day. I wanted to change jobs but without specialized skills I could only hope for an entry level position and there was no way to feed a family on minimum wage. Many evenings Marilyn and I would sit and talk about how I could possibly make a living some other way. On one such occasion we came to the end of our conversation as always, without any ray of hope. I got up from my seat and walked into our bedroom, wild with frustration and despair. Turning, I closed the door behind me by smashing my fist into it. The door still bears the marks of my knuckles in the plywood and it didn't do my hand a lot of good, either.

The Christian reader will wonder just where was my spirituality through all these years. I'm not proud of the attitudes I saw in myself and I wasn't much of a testimonial at times. I still read and studied the Scriptures although not as I should have, and I wanted to do right. But there were lessons to be learned and disciplines to be developed in my life that should have been learned in the first twenty years instead of the second. The older we get without learning to turn at His reproof, the bigger the rod the Lord has to use on us. That's one reason why I'm so concerned about training my children in Godly wisdom in their youth. I couldn't stand to see them endure the suffering I have brought on myself.

I did finally and gradually squirm out of the painting business. A friend suggested I look into doing fire restoration work for insurance companies and although I had grown understandably hesitant about friends' advice I talked to a few insurance people and got some jobs. Then of course I was faced with all kinds of work I didn't know how to do but I was beginning to learn how to learn. I asked around and found carpenters who could help me or do the work for me as subcontractors. The paint store people told me what primers to use to seal smoke stains. An insurance adjuster gave me a copy of one of his own estimates and I used the form and his unit prices to teach myself to bid. I never had the capital to really get into the restoration business but I made good money on a job now and then and learned more about learning. After a fire there are a number of different kinds of work to be done and I had opportunity to dabble in several.

Later I took a job building dormitories and other buildings at the college I had attended in 1975. The job was classified as temporary so there were no benefits but the pay was good. The uncertain length of employment also meant that it was hard for them to find the number of people they needed to complete the project on time. That made it easier for inexperienced people to land a job. I stayed there for nearly a year and picked up more skills though still not enough to be considered a pro at carpentry, concrete or any of the other trades at which I worked. A side benefit of the job was that there was a lot of overtime, meaning a big boost to the paycheck.

Yes, They're All Ours

I was one of the last temp's laid off, but my time finally came and wouldn't you know it was just about Christmas time. More painting followed (oh, joy), but less than a year afterwards the college called me back for another temporary project. This job proved to be my ticket out of painting purgatory.

We were remodeling a supermarket building into office space for the college and related enterprises, so there were a tremendous number of partition walls to be built in dividing the building into the desired rooms. I never would have been rehired for the carpentry work, because it was winter time and plenty of more experienced carpenters were looking for jobs. But all the partitioning involved a lot of drywall and as I had had more experience in that line than had most carpenters, I talked my former boss into accepting my offer of a position as my employer once again.

It was fortunate for me that, as before, there was a tight deadline to be met. This resulted in overtime work, meaning I could live on the pay. It also resulted in the fact that there was far too much drywall finishing for one man and we had to subcontract some expert help from outside. The boss called one drywall contractor and he came out to look at the work but the requirements of a Christian college were just too stringent for him. No smoking or bad language was permitted in the building.

Finally, the boss came to me and asked if I knew any drywall finishers. His carpenters could put the stuff up he said, but other than myself he didn't have any men who had done much finishing. As it happened, I had met a man through home education who was a drywall finisher by trade and was just setting up in business locally. I called him, he and the boss made an agreement and soon his men were on the job. I worked side by side for the first time with skilled drywall men.

Yes, They're All Ours

By now you know my style. It won't surprise you that in just a few weeks I was an expert finisher and ready to go out contracting drywall work on my own.

Actually, I didn't intend to do it exactly that way. When the office project was over and I got laid off again, I went to work for a home building company as a drywall finisher but got fired after a month because I didn't have enough experience.

Now I had to take the bull by the horns and go for the big time because I had eight children and no regular job for which I was qualified would support us. I got out the phone book and called every building contractor in the Yellow Pages. I got a few of them to give me a chance and managed to satisfy enough of them that I could keep going. I was slow and less than polished, but in drywall that which you lack in finesse you can partly compensate for with sandpaper and sweat.

Let me explain about drywall. First, you've probably heard it referred to as Sheetrock. Drywall is gypsum wallboard, Sheetrock is one brand of the product. Drywall is like aspirin, Sheetrock is like Bayer. The stuff comes in big sheets four feet wide, usually half an inch thick and in various lengths. The common length used in our area is twelve feet. The stuff is quite heavy, a twelve-foot sheet weighing nearly a hundred pounds. The process of putting drywall sheets up on the walls and ceiling with nails, screws and glue is called hanging (none of this will be on the exam). The procedure of covering the cracks ('joints') with paper tape and smoothing them with compound (informally known as mud) is referred to as finishing.

I couldn't do the hanging without help and at any rate I had learned that there was better money to be made in the finishing end. So I found some hangers to subcontract that end of the operation and concentrated on learning to finish. I worked it out with my customers to pay me immediately when the job was finished and with my hangers to be paid when I was paid. As do most drywall contractors in this town, I contract labor only and let the builder supply the materials. All this makes drywall a very inexpensive business to enter. Fortunately.

My scrambling entry to the drywall contracting business has now been seven years ago. It's not at all an easy business because of a number of variables which there's no need to discuss here. Suffice it to say that we've seen good times and hard times. Some months we've had too much work and strained to get it done. At other times we've been hard up for business and had to learn to go after it by phone canvassing builders and sending out promotional letters with humorous post cards, something I've never seen another contractor do. Like Miracle Maintenance, Boyer Drywall has been a real education. The main difference is that I've made a living at it.

Because we home educate, our sons have been free to work in the business with me. My two oldest boys, now nineteen and eighteen have worked with me since their preteen years and are skilled tradesmen. Either of them could make a good living in his own drywall business. They also know enough about the estimating and other management tasks that they could run such a business. They haven't made as much money helping to support the family as they would have by now had they worked elsewhere but they have a vocational education I didn't have when I was twice their age. Now they are capable of paying for a college education, supporting a family, starting their own business or whatever. They have a trade and they have good sense, neither of which I had starting out.

So my sons have not been losers in being partners with me and their help has made it possible for me to support the rest of the family. In fact when in 1991 my truck was struck in the rear end by a larger truck, permanently injuring my back, it was my boys who saved the day. The insurance company didn't treat us fairly and I expected our income to be drastically reduced the following year because of my impairment. Thanks to the efforts of my boys, it went up instead of down.

Nowadays they and their siblings also help Marilyn and me in the work of producing books and seminars on home education, which we feel is our family's true calling and which we hope to pursue full-time in the future (you can help facilitate that by encouraging all your friends to buy a copy of this book). I know my younger children will have to be told the story of my early years of struggle and the lessons I learned in providing for my family. But my big boys remember enough from their own experience to make them thankful that they will start out in adult life as wiser men than the one I was. I'm thankful too.

FAMILY SNAPSHOTS
Part V

We had gotten Rickey a new Bible for a special occasion and everybody was happy except three-year-old Tim.

"I want a new Bible, too!" He was never shy about letting his wants be known.

He could have had a new Bible too if he'd had a little patience but he wanted something done immediately.

"Tell you what, Tim," I said. "How about you get the Bible Rickey used to have? It was Daddy's before I gave it to Rickey. Then you'll have a big Bible that used to be Daddy's and Rickey will have the new little one."

That suited Tim perfectly. A typical second born, nothing would please him more than to have something bigger than what his older brother had. The fact that the big Bible had once been Dad's was a bonus.

The book in question was an old Bible given to me years before. I wasn't crazy about the version and hadn't used it much. It was old and tattered and beginning to fall apart. But Tim was proud of it even though he couldn't read a word of the text. Next Sunday he carried it to church.

"Hey, Pastor!" the little man called out to the preacher. "See my new Bible?"

"Oh, do you have a new Bible, Tim?" the pastor responded with enthusiasm.

"Yeah," Tim said, smiling and holding it up. "It used to be Rickey's *old* Bible but now it's my *new* Bible!"

Chapter 6

AND YOU HOME SCHOOL, TOO?

The decision to educate our children at home was one of the very best we ever made. We have never for a minute regretted doing so and all the dire predictions we heard from the naysayers in the early days have utterly failed to materialize. I feel that our children are having a happier, healthier childhood and being prepared for adult life far better than they could have been in an institution.

As I've told you before, we decided to home educate when we didn't know anybody ever did it. What started as a matter of convenience developed into a matter of conviction as we saw how well it worked for us. Learning came so simply and naturally as Marilyn gently led the boys along. Even now, with seven children in the classroom each day Marilyn never spends more than an hour and a half or so in teaching.

When we started out we didn't think much about the meaning of education in general. We hadn't developed a philosophy of learning because we didn't know we needed one. Our plan was just to get the kindergarten materials from our church's Christian school and work through them with the children in the order in which they were written. We assumed that the people who wrote the school books knew what our children needed to know and had put in the books.

As time went on we began to learn some simple lessons. We learned that there are more than one curriculum in the world. We learned that people learn from books that were never intended to be textbooks. We learned that different children learn in different ways and at different speeds. We learned that we could get good results without doing things just the way the curriculum writers intended.

These things hardly sound revolutionary now after fourteen years. But as I try to look back and see where we were in life then and how we saw things I don't feel too badly that we didn't start off on a bold, uncharted course right at the beginning. We've learned in baby steps but enough time has gone by that hopefully now we can condense many learning experiences into a concentrated form and give some help to others who can perhaps learn faster than those of us who started out by trial and error.

I have quite a list of lessons we've learned regarding educating our children. We don't know everything there is to know and even if we did there wouldn't be space enough in one chapter in one book to share it all. Besides, if I told you everything I know it would be hard to write any more books. But I would like to mention a few lessons that come to mind as some of the things we feel strongly about.

LESSON #1: SOME PEOPLE WON'T APPROVE

When we first decided not to send our boys to school any more we got quite excited. Marilyn loved teaching and I loved something different. I had always enjoyed doing things in a new and unusual way and I had also hated school. When I came to believe that we could educate our children without school there was a smug satisfaction in the thought that bordered on vengeance. So of course I was eager to tell people.

It didn't take me long to find out that broadcasting our intentions was not a good idea. Home education was unheard of to the public at that time and it seemed to smack of child neglect and babies locked in closets. When we told a friend back home about it he cautioned us about the danger of the children picking up our idiosyncrasies. At that time we didn't have a prepared response for that objection. Nowadays we just make it known that we don't think our idiosyncrasies are that much worse than the ones our children could pick up from their teachers and peers in school.

The average secularist will object to home education usually on logical grounds. He will either say that teaching is a complicated job requiring professional know-how or he'll express concern about the supposed lack of social contact. There has now been abundant research performed that shoots down the first argument; home educated students usually score far higher on standardized tests than their school counterparts who are taught by professionals. The socialization argument has been blown apart by research too, not to mention Scripture and experience. Yet it remains the most common objection we hear because most people aren't aware of what has been demonstrated through the studies. That's why we elected to write *The Socialization Trap* as our first book. We wanted to give home educators assurance that they are right and ammunition to defend their position.

The arguments you will hear from your Christian friends will not primarily be logical but rather emotional. The fact is you may very well get more flak from Christians than from anyone else. The problem is that any conviction that you have which they don't have is an automatic threat to them. They will either have to listen to your reasoning and consider whether it is something they should consider doing themselves or come up with all sorts of objections to show you just why you're all wet. Often it's much less threatening to attack someone else's conviction than to try it on for oneself. Your Christian friends may have any number of sensible-sounding arguments, but usually they're motivated by emotion more than logic.

As I say, we found early on that the less we said about our plan to home educate, the less time we wasted arguing with people who weren't listening.

LESSON #2: EDUCATION IS SIMPLE

Education really is simple. It's school that's complicated. For a mother to sit down with a phonics book and teach her child to read is a far cry from the classroom teacher who has twenty or thirty children all the same age and endless record keeping and other donkey work to take up her time.

Benjamin Franklin was one of the best educated men in our nation's history with accomplishments to his credit in the fields of literature, business, science, politics, education and economics. Yet he only went to school for two years and was not an outstanding student while there.

When his father could no longer afford his tuition, Ben was apprenticed to his older brother as a printer's helper. Ben had an inquiring mind and wanted to know more than he did about a wide range of subjects. He worked out an agreement with his brother by which he would buy his own lunch every day rather than eating at their boarding house at midday. This would save his brother some money, as he was paying room and board for the apprentice. Ben asked that in return his brother give to him half the money saved, with which he then bought his own lunch (usually a biscuit or a handful of raisins) and spent the rest on books. Young Franklin then had books to read and the midday break on which to read them.

When he found that he didn't know enough arithmetic to handle some of the clerical responsibilities of his position, he bought an arithmetic book and worked himself through it. And so it went with other topics as well. When Ben discovered a new interest or found that he needed to know something he didn't know, he got his hands on a book or sought out someone who knew more than he did about the subject.

Lest you fear that you're not smart enough to do for your children what Ben Franklin did for himself, relax. School textbooks are very self-explanatory. They have to be because teachers have too many students to give each one very much personal attention.

As we got deeper into the home education experience we found that there's much more you can do than just working through books. There are all sorts of hands-on learning projects, experiments and field trips that make it all so interesting you'll wonder why any parent would let someone else have the joy of teaching his children for him.

LESSON #3: YOU CAN'T HOME EDUCATE IF YOU'RE NEVER HOME

Marilyn has always been a the type who likes home quite well, thank you, and doesn't feel any desire to run all around town all day instead of being at home with her children.. This, however seems to be more the exception than the rule among women her age. We've known women who go out shopping in the morning and get hungry so they go out for lunch at noon and gain weight so they go to the fitness center in the afternoon.

The syndrome affects home educating moms as well as others. Many mothers seem to feel that the more activities they can involve their children in, the more they will learn. This might be true if all activities were of equal value. But when Mom is little more than a taxi driver, carting this child to music lessons, that one to Little League and the other one to 4-H, her time is not being well spent. People seem to be so afraid their child will miss something that they keep him in the car all the time where he misses just about everything including the most important thing, time with Mom and the family.

We have found that for every activity or field trip that is worth attending, there are a dozen or more things of greater educational value that can be done at home with less time and effort.

LESSON #4: DON'T LET THE BOOKS BE THE BOSS

Books make wonderful servants but (with the exception of the Bible) rotten masters. We found out early on that textbooks and teacher's guides are written for schools, not for home education. This means that there is a lot of stuff in them that you won't need. Marilyn never buys a teacher's guide because she says they're useless. As for the textbooks themselves, let me offer a couple of examples.

Let's say a page in the fourth grade math book contains five story problems and twenty practice problems written in numerals only. If your child works the story problems and gets them all correct, he may not need any more practice. But because those practice problems are there, I would at one time have assumed that it was because someone had done some research and found that that much repetition was needed.   Not so. We eventually figured out that those extra problems are there so that the children who are behind the others can have plenty of practice and the faster children have enough seat work to keep them busy so they're not finding creative ways to otherwise pass the time. Far better to let them use the time allotted to move on to the next page and start on a new skill level. Some home educated kids who like numbers complete two or three "grades" worth of math in a single year.

Yes, They're All Ours

I was interested to read a comment by a schoolteacher who said she had noticed that some children could do three or five math problems of a certain level of difficulty and get them all correct, but when faced with a whole page full of them would get nervous and make mistakes. Some children, she said, would be so intimidated they would burst into tears even though they had already demonstrated the necessary proficiency to do the work. If children like these were taught at home, their parents could give them the individual attention needed to see that they got enough practice without it becoming an ordeal. The writer of the textbook could not know each individual child's needs.

I once visited a small Christian school and sat with a teacher as six students worked math problems on the blackboard. He pointed out to me that even in a group so small, two students were staying right with the teacher's verbal instructions, two children were a step ahead and waiting on the others, and the remaining two were behind and needed extra help.

Another common occurrence of book bondage is in required writing. For instance, if the child has a reading assignment in a history book and there are review questions at the end of the section, often the curriculum guide or the book itself will call for the answers to the questions to be written out and submitted for the teacher's evaluation. Again, if a teacher has thirty students to evaluate writing may be the only feasible method. But at home the child can see that the writing is unnecessary. He can tell Mom the answers verbally much quicker than he can write them out. If she requires the writing just because the book calls for it, it can be pretty demotivating.

When we say this in a workshop, some parents object that children need to practice their writing. That's true of course, but I suggest a more interesting and productive

93

method, such as writing a note to a friend or relative or a letter to the editor. Writing things that do not need to be written is just the sort of mental masochism that makes moms and children burn out on home education.

We found out in the early years that it worked far better to make the books keep pace with us than to commit ourselves to keeping pace with the books. I think I've already told you about our son Rickey and his interest in history. When in first grade he read the fourth grade history book cover to cover, eight times. In school he would not have been allowed to do that, perhaps causing as much frustration as being forced along at too fast a pace. Parents need to develop the confidence to tailor the curriculum to the child. One size does not fit all.

LESSON #5: LEARNING IS FUN

I left secondary school with a rotten taste in my mouth. I was sick and tired of being coerced into memorizing a lot of data I cared nothing about then being tested to see how completely I could regurgitate it. I had been a very inquisitive child but by the time I graduated from high school the combination of school regimentation and TV addiction had stunted my ability to wonder. My subsequent exposure to the real world with its real needs and opportunities has at least begun to rebuild my lost faculties, but I don't think I'll ever again have that childlike fascination with my environment, wanting to know what everything is and how it works.

Marilyn was more suited to schooling than I was and made excellent grades, but she tells me that nearly everything she memorized for a test, she forgot right away. We have since found that learning sticks better if it's enjoyable and useful rather than part of a jump-through-the-hoop behavior exercise motivated by grades as sticks and carrots.

First of all, there are things we need to learn that almost no one really enjoys learning. For instance, math facts. Some children enjoy the challenge of rote memorization but for most people it's drudgery. Still, we must know the multiplication tables to move past a certain point in math basics. When faced with necessary drudgery, Marilyn tries to find some way to make it more interesting. Rewards have worked well in this; most children if not forced along too fast will respond to the promise of some sort of goody at the end of the project. We have several fish tanks in our home and all the children like fish. So Marilyn may set some goal for the child, perhaps so many math facts recited in so many minutes. When you can do it Mom will take you down to the pet store and you can pick out a new fish. Incidentally, the fish sense the importance of this and cooperate by constantly dying so there's always room for new inmates.

Most learning is not drudgery and doesn't require challenges and treats. Humans are born learners, as babies demonstrate. As soon as they get old enough to crawl around they're into everything. Climbing, reaching, pawing, gnawing. They want to know how everything, no matter how common looks, feels, sounds and tastes. Most of us don't lose this hunger for discovery until we go to school and are confined in desks so we can't explore. Then we are frustrated by the twin devils of forced assimilation/regurgitation and curiosity that we have no means to satisfy. I heard a fifth-grade teacher wonder aloud why adults can't talk fast enough to answer a five-year-old's questions, yet by the time he enters fifth grade he practically has to have a hole knocked in his head to get any information poured in. The answer, of course is all the schooling that takes place in the five years between the two ages. As

95

practiced in modern America, education is the enemy of learning.

Children need to pursue their interests. Interests can be a tremendous key to learning if we just don't stifle them. Rickey's interest in politics has been a real education for Marilyn and me. As he has read the publications, gone to the meetings, listened to the radio programs, watched the videos, the political interest has led to learning in other areas as well. You can't talk politics and not talk economics, history, geography, current events, science and on and on. And not only has the one interest led the one son into other interests, but the other children's exposure to politics through their older brother's involvement has caused them to get interested as well. It works on parents, too. I was never a delegate to a political convention until my son led me into it. Now I'm getting the education they failed to give me in government class.

Another key to enjoyable learning is the presence of Mom and/or Dad. Children like to be near their parents if the relationships are in good health and this makes for good home learning. One day Marilyn gave out assignments in the dining room where the children usually do their required book work, then retired to the living room to fold some laundry. Within five minutes one of the kids was in on the sofa working away in his book. Soon another drifted in with his work, then another and another until soon everybody was in the living room. No one spoke to Mommy; they just wanted to be near her. If children sense the need for Mom's presence, think how motivated they must be by her active involvement. I tell beginners that the essence of home education is the parent-child relationship. That's why I have little use for correspondence home schools and less for video systems. Don't major on doing things *for* your children but *with* your children. We've found that kids are much more interested in a book, lesson or project if one or both parents demonstrate their own interest by their involvement.

LESSON #6: LEARNING AT HOME KEEPS FAMILIES CLOSE

Marilyn and I have been saddened over the years as we've observed families who drifted apart. One man told me that he had worked hard for years to be able to afford a house at the lake and time to relax there, and when he finally got to that point his wife and children had developed outside pursuits and had little interest in the lake house.

Home education is not a guarantee that this won't happen and schooling is not a curse that insures that it will. But we believe that the more effort parents put into the family, the more the children will respond. We have known home educators who were seldom home. They wore themselves out taking the children here and there for this or that social or intellectual experience (usually social) and one day woke up to find that their children had little interest in what was going on at home.

Marilyn's parents did not educate her at home, but they were very family oriented people. Nearly all of their recreation centered around their family. They didn't go out a lot without the children and when they had groups over to the house it was usually relatives. Marilyn loved being home.

Today she still loves to be home, although we have a hard time carrying on an uninterrupted conversation and so often end up going out on dinner dates. But you can see the fruit of her philosophy in her children. Other than the older boys who are working jobs, politicking and otherwise moving into their places in the adult world, the children like to be home. And though they are home a lot and enjoy an outing very much, home is not a place they find restrictive an uninteresting. They have not fallen victim to the youth subculture that sucks children out of their families and adopts them into the age peer tribe.

FAMILY SNAPSHOTS
Part V

I've coined a few special terms in referring to parts of the children's bodies.

When Josh got a fish bone stuck down in his throat I had to reach far down in there to grasp it with a pair of tissue forceps and pull it out.

"Well, Schweetness, that thing was stuck plumb crossways in your gizzard!"

Whenever we return from being out in public as a family Marilyn drafts me to help run through the lineup washing faces and hands to remove any gunk or germs.

"Stand still, honey, and let Daddy scrub yer mug and paws."

It was when Mattie was a fat little three-year-old, our only pudgy baby so far, that I was inspired with a term for his thighs. We were stopped in a restaurant while traveling on vacation and Matt was eating an ice cream cone but not quite quickly enough when we noticed he was starting to whimper.

"What's the matter, honey?" Marilyn asked.

Matt was a very sensitive little boy. His lower lip trembled as he answered.

"Ice cream just dripped on my hams!"

Chapter 7

ON HAVING IT ALL TOGETHER

My only claim to fame is that I have twelve children and don't color my hair. I never claimed to be smarter than anyone else and certainly not any more spiritual. My wife and I are just well-meaning parents of a larger-than-ordinary family. So where do people get the idea that we never have any problems?

Marilyn and I have both had it happen. Some mom or dad comes up to one of us after a talk at a seminar or convention and says, "Boy, you guys sound like you really have it all together."

We do?

I've formulated a theory. Since this normally happens at speaking engagements, it must be in response to the fact that we usually have answers ready when people ask us questions at the end of a talk. Don't let that fool you. The simple fact is that we hear the same questions over and over because parents share pretty much the same concerns. So we've had years to work on solutions to the most common problems. And when some parent pops up with a question so narrow that it obviously speaks only to their family's situation, nobody expects us to pull a quick answer out of the hat. Either way, we get more credit than we deserve.

Lest any of my readers have ever gotten the impression that the Boyers "have it all together" (or think they do) and never struggle as do other families, let me share some news with you that you may find encouraging. We have the same problems you do. In fact, some of those problems are multiplied in our family because of the numbers involved.

So if you think that omniscience is a prerequisite to having a large family, think again.

Some of our challenges are obvious. For instance, have you ever cooked a meal for fourteen people? If I hadn't experienced the blessing of KP in the military, I wouldn't have believed they even make pots and pans big enough. Then when you've collected enough utensils, there aren't enough cabinets in the kitchen to hold everything. Nor is there a residential type refrigerator that will contain enough food once we've made one of our frequent shopping trips. And of course those shopping trips are painful in another way too. Our grocery bill looks like the national debt.

Food isn't the only expense. In fact, when people ask me how I can afford twelve children, the answer is simple. I can't. It's a good thing Marilyn and I didn't follow the conventional wisdom and wait until we could afford children before having them. I'd be a lonely old man today. Were it not for my wife's expert management, I'd have to own a gold mine.

We seem to use tons of everything. Most likely, we eat more food than your family, buy more clothes than your family and, thanks to the fact that I'm self-employed and have to pay all my own social security, we just might pay more taxes than your family, too.

No doubt the environmental radicals would consider us earth-trashers. We drive big vehicles, both for carrying capacity and safety considerations. We burn lots of gas and plenty of firewood. As a matter of fact, if trees ever take over the world we may be in big trouble. Our toilet paper consumption alone is probably enough to account for the untimely death of some innocent giant sequoia. And if you could compute our total paper consumption in paper towels, plates, diapers, tissues and school materials, it would probably account for the demise of the Sahara Forest. (Yes, I know it's the Sahara *Desert*. Now.)

Have you ever wondered what it's like to do our laundry? Dwelling on the thought could cause nightmares. We've gone through enough detergent to put a thick head of suds on the entire South Pacific. Five loads a day is average. Recovering from a day or two of down time for washer repairs has brought Marilyn as close to the brink of suicide as I've ever seen her. True, the children are trained to help with the washing, but Marilyn still has her share of the work and when something is lost, damaged or mismatched the owner comes running to Mom. I recall one night about eleven p.m. when I was moaning about how tired I was after a long day on the job. I was in the middle of an intense self-pity session when Marilyn walked into the room carrying a basket of clothes which she set down on the floor in front of the sofa and began to fold. I subsided.

I don't think there's a house in the world designed for a family the size of ours. If there is, it doubtless has Hilton on a sign out front. We are constantly remodeling to fit another child in a bedroom or create more storage space. When we got a building permit to enclose the carport we learned why our drains back up every time it rains. It seems when the house was built, the excavators ran into solid rock in the back yard and were unable to put in as much drain field as usual. So even our septic system is too small All we have to do now is have new drain fields dug in the less rocky uphill parts of our property, which doesn't entail much besides a three-thousand-dollar pump-up septic system. Contributions may be sent to me in care of STINKAID.

Then there are the human relations problems jus as in your family, but multiplied by whatever number is applicable. I sometimes don't know if I'm a father, referee, police officer or zoo keeper. I can't say my life is easy, but at least I don't often get bored.

We have our little misunderstandings. Nobody ever starts it, you understand; it just starts. Once Josh ordered some nasty-looking, sea-dwelling creatures called blood worms to feed his tropical fish. They came frozen in blocks and he kept the disgusting things in our refrigerator freezer. When little sister Carrie saw him for the first time go to the freezer for a chunk and asked him what he was doing, he explained that he was after some blood worms. She didn't understand and thought she was missing out on some fine frozen confection. Her wail of protest filled the house: "They're not all for you!"

Along with disagreements, the other usual problems of humanity are ever present too. The ordeal of getting everybody dressed for church should qualify Marilyn for sainthood. It would never do for a shoe to be where it's expected to be. And as for fixing the hair of five little girls ages two to ten...I'm considering crew cuts for the entire family.

Sometimes life in the large family gets a little bewildering. Occasionally it's hard to tell who's here and who's not. We once drove off and left Katie at the city library by herself. And quiet little Nathan once accidentally stayed at church while the rest of the family piled into the station wagon and headed off to the supermarket on the way home. When we discovered our mistake and went back looking for him, Nate was gone and so was everyone else. We assumed he had caught a ride and sure enough, when we arrived at home there were some of our friends in the driveway with Nathan in the back seat and big grins on their faces.

More children generally mean more medical problems. Our doctor tells us we're the healthiest family seen at her office, but I'm sure the sheer number of us guarantees college funds for at least two of the doctor's children.

Our greatest medical crisis occurred when Katie, then eight hears old, nearly died with a ruptured appendix. I spent nights with her for the entire week she was in the hospital while continuing to work every day. When she came home, I was exhausted and she was suffering from occasional attacks of sever stomach pain probably caused by the nasal tube that had drained her stomach for several days in the hospital. Every parent knows the agony of getting up at night to try to comfort a child when nothing can be done for the pain. One night I was up with Katie several times interspersed with visits to the bedside of another sick child, leaving me physically and emotionally shot and wanting nothing more than to just lie down and quietly expire. As I collapsed back into bed after one of these nocturnal torture sessions, I moaned piteously to Marilyn, "Whose idea was it to have children?" It became a standard saying and now when the pressure is on and we feel ourselves approaching meltdown it's not unusual for one of us to whimper the abbreviated form: "Whose idea was it...?"

Such times are a part of life in any family. And having six times the number of children in the average American family, I suppose I should expect a larger share. It comes with the territory. There is of course no malice in most of the challenges children provide for their parents; some of the problems are acts of God and some are just the result of kids being kids.

I once made the mistake of leaving three-year-old Tim in the car for a couple of minutes while I got out and talked to a neighbor. I came back to find my dashboard the apparent victim of a machine gun attack. Tim had been experimenting with a screwdriver.

When we had just bought our house and were remodelling prior to moving in, the children found it hard to discern which things we wanted to change and which should be left alone. Five-year-old Nathan took initiative and added what he deemed an important customizing feature in the expensive chair rail molding in the master bedroom. I stopped him just short of a full circuit of the room, making hatchet cuts at fairly regular three-inch intervals.

Through the years a sense of humor has been indispensable. We haven't always kept it, but somehow we've always managed to regain it. Marilyn is the heroine of it all. She has gone through pregnancy gracefully, even the latter stages when though she looks very good she feels as if she should have WIDE LOAD printed on her back, GOODYEAR stamped on her stomach and suspenders on her pantyhose. She goes through labors which are not particularly easy ones, then caring for the infant and the toddler and finally, the teenager. I never cease to admire the loving way in which she weathers the storms of motherhood. Day after day, year after year she bears up faithfully under challenges that would soon have me taking up residence in a quiet rubber room somewhere. Don't get me wrong; there are plenty of good times too. In fact it's not a circus around here most of the time. Just often enough to keep us humble.

If you're one of those who assume that moms and dads of large families must have some special powers or if you're hoping to find and emulate some perfect parents I'm afraid you'll have to look elsewhere. There's nobody in here but us humans.

That said, you may wonder why we do it. Why do people continue to have babies at an age when most of their contemporaries are getting their children through high school and looking forward to retirement and easier times? The answer is simple: Though added children bring added challenges, they bring added blessings as well. And throughout the years, whether in our early days of parenthood or more recent times when our quiver appears to be getting full, we look around at our family and feel exactly the way you do about yours. We just don't see anybody there we think we could live without.

FAMILY SNAPSHOTS
Part VI

On our honeymoon I took my new bride to visit my grandparents in the country. Grandad had always been my favorite relative because he was a real old original hillbilly. Now it had been a year or two since I had seen him. He was getting on in years and I was always concerned when I visited him that I might find him physically or mentally declining.

When we arrived at the farm Grandad got up from his seat on the porch and shuffled across the yard as we were getting out of the car. He didn't say much to me because Grandad always acted as if he'd seen me just the week before regardless of how long it had actually been.

"Hi, Grandad!" I exclaimed. I was always glad to see Grandad. "This is my wife, Marilyn. Honey, this is my grandad, Mr. E.O. Tucker."

Grandad and Marilyn greeted each other cordially then the old man looked back at me.

"Is 'at the same gal you's with yesterday?"

I took a sharp breath. So that's how it was. Grandad's mind was going. I hadn't even been in the state yesterday.

Just then my brother and his girlfriend came driving up the dirt road and stopped in the driveway beside where we stood. Grandad looked in the car at Dean then at the young lady, then back at Dean and spoke. And then I was relieved to learn that old Grandad hadn't changed a bit.

"Is 'at the same gal you's with yesterday?"

Chapter 8

WHY SO MANY?

Actually, it was just as well that they transferred me out of the boys' home economics class my senior year. All I can remember learning in there was how to shave and I didn't even need to know that yet. But it was an interesting quirk of fate that I should then find myself in Biology II shooting craps.

Well, it wasn't exactly that way, but we were rolling dice. The school had moved me out of one class into another because I lacked a science credit needed for graduation and now I found myself tumbling the little dotted cubes around on a black formica countertop with two lab partners, wondering how such an activity ever came to be deemed scientific.

Evidently I wasn't the first kid ever to be confused about the proper application of dice. My dad and his brother as children once asked a younger boy in their country neighborhood if he ever shot craps.

"No," he answered in mild disgust. "If I did, Mama wouldn't cook 'em."

The purpose of the dice was to demonstrate the effect of chance on sex selection. The teacher had explained a deep and wondrous mathematical concept to us which was supposed to be illustrated by the dice. He had told us that since there are two sexes, the chances that one individual would be born male was one in two or fifty per cent. Coincidentally, the chances were the same that the individual would be born female.

Now we were rolling the dice on the counter and noting in columns the comparative count of odd and even numbers

108

rolled. Even numbers represented male births, odd numbers stood for females. After the designated time had elapsed, the teacher called for our totals. I don't remember any of the lab teams getting an exactly even count, although maybe some of them did. As a matter of fact I didn't even pay much attention to the score our lab team ended up with.. There was no money riding on the dice and I've never really been fascinated with numbers.

Looking back through a lens now twenty-five years thick the exercise is clouded with ambiguity, but I think what they were trying to teach us was that our gender is an accident. That would seem to be a reasonable conclusion because much of the class time throughout the entire year had been spent teaching us that the whole human race was an accident. Humanity was a product of evolution, the book said. The end result of an ages-long chain of coincidences.

That was in 1969. Evolution had been firmly engrafted into our educational system for many years and so we should perhaps have been less surprised when four years later the Supreme Court declared that an unborn American baby could be separated from his right to life by a barrier no thicker than his mother's abdominal wall.

A quarter of a century after the scientific dice-rolling of Biology II I find myself the progenitor of fourteen human lives, twelve of whom are with me, two of whom are in heaven by means of miscarriage and none of whom are accidents. A time or two when a couple of our babies arrived unusually close together chronologically, we were asked something like, "Only fifteen months apart! Was this planned?" You bet your life it was planned.

All births are planned, whether people know anything about it or not. Ecclesiastes 3 makes it clear that there is a time to be born and a time to die. We believe those times are ordained by God.

Yes, They're All Ours

As you've read in an earlier chapter, Marilyn and I entered upon marriage without really thinking through our position on birth control. "Everybody" waited to have children, so we would wait. I don' t recall discussing in any depth the number of children we would have either, but I seem to recall having the number four in mind, I suppose because I myself had three siblings so that seemed a normal family.

We were probably less than six months into our marriage when one evening after work I burst in through the front door of our apartment and without preamble commanded my wife, "Woman, throw away those pills!"

I don't recall her exact response, but she must have wondered what had gotten into me. I explained that I had decided we should have a child. A little boy had come in that day to the pediatric clinic at the Air Force hospital where I was working as a medical corpsman and stolen my heart. He was a little tiny guy about three years old and dressed up like a small adult. He had a big smile and dimples but I don't remember much else as there has been a long procession of cute kids through my life in the intervening years. I do clearly remember thinking when I saw him, "I gotta get me one of those things!"

And I got one. Something less than a year later I was the proud papa of a lively baby boy. Rickey was still an infant when I awoke to the fact that birth control was without a sound apologetic in Christian doctrine, delivering him from any danger of growing up an only child.

The college class mentioned earlier was the springboard for my thoughts. Then as Marilyn and I talked about it and began to search the Scriptures a bit, we grew more and more convinced that we had been wrong in trying at all to plan our family. We came to the conclusion that family planning is God's job.

The first thing we noticed in Scripture is that children are always referred to as a blessing. Psalm 127:3 says,

Lo, children *are* an heritage of the LORD: *and* the fruit of the womb *is His* reward.

Rewards are given for accomplishment. They are looked upon as just compensation for a person's actions. That means that you deserve the children you have (some people must find that a chilling thought).

I can just hear the objections: "Wait a minute. Do you mean that if a child is conceived through adultery that God has chosen to reward adultery?"

Not at all. I'm saying that if a woman becomes pregnant through adultery and delivers the child, she is being rewarded for giving birth when she knows that the child will always be a reminder to her and to others of her sin. She is being rewarded for not aborting the child to hide her guilt even though it is legal to do so.

But most children are not conceived through adultery. Even in our debauched day when unbelievable numbers of babies are being born out of wedlock, the majority still come into the homes of married couples. And it is to those couples, specifically Christian couples, that this chapter is addressed.

If you're a Christian parent, you will already recognize that children are a blessing. True, there are some attendant hassles, such as loud noises and unpleasant smells. But most blessings bring with them some small liabilities. Just think-- if you were a millionaire people would always be trying to borrow money from you. Yet if I offered you a million dollars as a gift, all the moochers probably wouldn't cause you to turn it down.

Yes, They're All Ours

Let's look again at Psalm 127. Note verse 4:

As arrows *are* in the hand of a mighty man; so *are* the children of the youth.

What are arrows? First of all, they're an offensive weapon. Eph. 6:16 tells us that faith is our shield; that's our defensive weapon. Arrows are not to protect us from the enemy's attack, but to launch an attack of our own. Too many Christians see spiritual warfare as a defensive battle when in fact God wants us on the offensive. Remember Jesus told Peter in Matt. 16:18 that the gates of hell would not prevail against the church. Gates are defensive in nature, not offensive. Satan isn't going to jerk the gates of hell off their hinges and go around bashing Christians over the head with them. God wants us not just to be alert to Satan's attacks but to launch attacks of our own.

Scripture talks about several offensive weapons. There is the sword, for close combat. Then there is the spear, which can travel a certain distance or be used in close-up fighting as well. It's the arrow that has the longest range, along with a high degree of accuracy.

This is the thing that comes to my mind when I think of my children as arrows. I hold them in my hand for a while. I shelter them from the elements in my quiver, I make them myself and sharpen and straighten them. Then when the time comes to launch them they are prepared to strike targets that are far beyond my own reach.

King David, mighty man of valor that he was still had one target he wanted to strike before his life was over. His heart's desire was to build a temple for the Lord. But in I Ch. 17 God told David that that particular target was beyond his reach. The temple was built, but it was built by David's son, King Solomon after the death of David. David had not

112

accomplished his goal in close combat but his arrow reached the target even when David was no longer on the scene.

I like the sound of that. In my life there are many things I would like to do for the Lord but which I will never accomplish. It's good to know that there are at least twelve children coming after me, all of whom I hope will be spiritually stronger than I ever was, are better educated and have more years left to serve God. Already my children can do important things that I can't do. I look forward to the future because I'm eager to see my arrows strike deep in the Lord's targets, accomplishing things for Him that are far beyond my reach.

Arrows are not guided missiles. Once they're launched there are no remote controls by which we can steer them. But if the archer is skillful he will have his arrows in good condition and aim them properly, taking the windage into account and putting plenty of force behind them so they're harder to deflect.

Psalm 127:5 tells us more:

Happy *is* the man that hath his quiver full of them: they shall not be ashamed, but they shall speak with the enemies in the gate.

How big is a quiver? This question has been bandied about thousands of times, usually in my experience in an attempt to find loopholes. I've heard it said that the quiver referred to here is a hunting quiver holding perhaps four or five arrows. I have a problem with that explanation because in the previous verse it makes clear the fact that the arrows referred to are in the hand of a 'mighty man". The Hebrew word translated into the phrase 'mighty man' is usually used in reference to a soldier. In fact in this verse the New American Standard Bible translates it 'warrior'. The King

James translates it as here, 'mighty man' or 'mighty one' a total of 139 times. It is almost always in a context of war and soldier life.

For that reason I suggest that the quiver in question is not for hunting with a measley four or five arrows but rather a war quiver. How many arrows did they hold? I don't know, but if I were an archer in a battle I'd want a lot more than four or five shots.

Another interesting aspect of the quiver-and-arrows analogy that occurred to me is this: If your quiver is crammed with arrows, it's hard for any of them to fall out. I noticed as a boy when bowhunting that if I only had two arrows in a quiver that would hold a dozen they would rattle around and threaten to come out when I ran. Does this prove that large families tend to be closer? That might be a bit of a stretch, but I do feel that the teamwork necessary in a family the size of ours generates a bonding influence. Daily life reminds us over and over again that we are all needed and needing each other.

I also feel that there is a significance to the last part of verse 5 where it says that they shall speak with the enemies in the gate. This refers to the city gates, where in ancient times important business was conducted. It was in the gates of the city that important legal cases were decided and councils of war held. The verse here seems to me to indicate that the children of the full quiver are those who end up in important positions in the community. Why would this be?

Contrary to what institutionalists say, the best social experience for children is not to be had in school but at home. At school the child can pick and choose among companions and avoid those who irritate him. Supervision is loose so a lot of bullying can go on as well. If you don't like somebody, you can try to stay away from him or even threaten and intimidate him. On the other hand if a more powerful person doesn't like you, you could be in trouble. Social relationships in school, moreover are influenced by the artificial rankings of students as "better" or "worse" in academics, athletics, etc., so that success is based on competition.

At home it's different. The daily relationships are close, intense and perpetual. You can't just avoid those who rub you the wrong way; you have to learn to compromise preferences and live together. Because all members need each other, success is not based on competition but on cooperation. If the children fail, the parents have failed. If one fails, the group suffers.

In our family we have to learn to adjust to a large number of different personality types because a large number of them live in the same house. Can it be that the children of the full quiver have better people skills than others and therefore are called upon to negotiate complicated and important matters?

In looking up the many verses about children in Scripture I saw an unmistakable pattern emerge: Children are a blessing and the subject of many promises. Never are they referred to as a curse, as some modern people seem to view them.

I have said before that most great blessings entail some small liabilities. Today we seem to have confused the blessing with the liability. For instance, children are a blessing. When Adam and Eve sinned they were told that through childbearing a Savior would come to the world. But it was also at that point that clothing came into the world. Prior to that time nobody had ever done laundry.

Now let's look at this thing in context. Childbearing was the road to salvation. That's blessing. Laundry was the direct result of sin. That's a curse. With babies come laundry but it's the laundry, not the baby, that is the curse.

Yes, They're All Ours

In Genesis 1:28 God told Adam and Eve (constituting at that time the entire human race) to "Be fruitful and multiply, and fill the earth, and subdue it." When did He rescind that order?

It wasn't in Genesis 9:1-7, where He told Noah and his sons to go forth and "'multiply" and replenish the earth. Nor was it in Genesis chapters 17 and 22 where He promised to multiply Abraham. Nor was it in Genesis 26, Genesis 35, Leviticus 26, or Jeremiah 33. It was in those chapters that God promised as a blessing to *multiply* Isaac, then Jacob, then the nation of Israel, then David. If God was so often promising to multiply families and even nations as a blessing, where do modern Christian get the idea that fewer is better in relation to children? The idea doesn't come from God.

Some time ago I ran into an acquaintance, a young Christian lady who had been a newlywed the last time I had seen her some years before. She had a little girl with her whom I assumed was hers. But she said, "No, this is one of my students. Dave and I plan to have children later on, but we're having too much fun right now."

Strange that we should treat life so casually. Strange too, that childrearing should be considered the antithesis of fun. I can't imagine anything more fun than watching some of the antics of the little people around my house.

But nowadays children, and especially in large numbers, seem to be regarded as a liability; more a curse than a blessing. Margaret Sanger, founder of Planned Parenthood, once said that the kindest thing the parents of a large family could do for their youngest child was to kill it. In the early part of the century, when she started her crusade for life prevention, Sanger was repeatedly jailed for distributing literature and opening clinics to combat fruitfulness. It was illegal at that time to encourage contraception. How things have changed. Now in China women pregnant with even their second child are given forced abortions.

It is barrenness, not fruitfulness that is to be deplored. This is not to say that a woman who cannot have children is sinning or loved less by God than one who is a mother. A child born without some other physical capacity such as sight or hearing is not to be criticized either, but blindness and deafness were conditions from which people came to Jesus to seek healing. They are not spoken of in Scripture as rewards. Again, I want to emphasize that I'm not saying that a woman to whom God has not given a husband or a couple to whom God has not given children is less valuable to God or has necessarily done anything wrong. I'm just trying to call attention to the fact that modern American believers have their values turned around.

The closed womb was historically viewed as a liability and in some cases evidence of God's curse. In Genesis 20, for instance, the king of Gerar, a man called Abimelech took Abraham's wife, Sarah for his harem. God came to him in a dream and told him to restore the woman on pain of death. Abimelech gave Sarah back to Abraham and Abraham prayed to God to remove the punishment that had already befallen Abimelech's household. What was the punishment? Verses 17 and 18 tell us:

And Abraham prayed to God; and God healed Abimelech and his wife and his maids, so that they bore *children*. For the LORD had closed fast all the wombs of the household of Abimelech because of Sarah, Abraham's wife.

When Elizabeth, mother of John the Baptist found out that she was pregnant after reaching the point of being "advanced in years" still barren, she said, **"This is the way**

the LORD has dealt with me in the days when He looked *with favor* **upon** *me,* **to take away my disgrace among men** (Lk. 1:25 NASV)." Today it is disgraceful to have children, or to have too many. In that day it was disgraceful not to have children.

Throughout the Bible, it was always clear that God loved human life and Satan hated it. God's plan for redemption of the race is the perpetuation of a godly seed. Not surprisingly, Satan's program has consistently one of trying to destroy the godly seed. Hence the drowning of the Hebrew baby boys in the Nile in the day of Pharaoh and the murder by Herod of all the boys under two years old in and around Bethlehem at the time Christ was born. The abortion business of today should be recognized as Satanic in origin. When people in hospitals and clinics, trained medical professionals, can look at a trash can full of tiny arms and legs and refer to 'products of conception' rather than murdered babies, the Deceiver has been hard at work.

He's been busy in the church, as a matter of fact. Attitudes toward childbearing among Christians aren't much closer to the principles of Scripture than among the earth people. We all decry abortion and yet we're so casual toward the issue of human life that we are willing to turn fertility on and off (especially off) like a water faucet. I am not looking to pick a fight with any believer who has honestly searched the Scriptures and come to the conclusion that we have the right to limit the size of our families. To his own Master he stands or falls, and God has the power to change the mind of whichever of us is wrong. It's those who are where I was at the time I got married that I would wrestle with, those who don't see the issue as important enough to warrant prayer and Bible study.

I've come to feel that most people do their family planning on the basis of selfishness. If you have all the children God sends to you without contraceptive interference your parental responsibilities will probably dominate your life. People realize that and so they rule out a large family usually before they even get married. We would all say that we wouldn't trade our children for anything in the world and yet that is precisely what we do with "our" children-- the ones we could have but refuse to receive. I wonder if there is a house in heaven where little boy and girl spirits live until bodies are made for them on earth. If there is such a home up there it must be full to overflowing because there's a tremendous housing shortage down here.

Marilyn and I have come to the opinion that none of the known methods of contraception are acceptable to us even if we had no philosophical objection. All the pharmaceutical and mechanical meddling with nature are frightening to us. An IUD is the implantation of a foreign body inside a woman. Vasectomy has been proven to be pathological. As for the method we used early on, the Pill, it's garbage.

The birth control pills Marilyn took when we were first married made a basket case of her. On our honeymoon when we were traveling around, doing things that should have been fun, she would suddenly start to cry. On one such occasion I got frustrated and asked her rather unsympathetically what was wrong. She didn't know. She just felt like crying. That was totally out of character for Marilyn. She hates to cry and hates to be in a bad mood. She's definitely not one of those women who are never happy without something to be unhappy about. It wasn't until we decided to toss the pills that we found out why she had been so melancholy. The strong hormones in the pills evidently were devastating to her emotions. As if our first months of marriage weren't hard enough for her already.

We found out only after several years and several children that we may very well be guilty of abortion because of the

119

pill. The pill is intended to keep a sperm cell from fertilizing the egg cell. Sometimes, however, this fails to happen and the pill performs its secondary function of keeping the fertilized egg from implanting in the placenta wall, causing the cell to die. If you believe as I do that life begins at conception, then use of the birth control pill is inviting abortion.

Besides all that, we have known a number of women who were unable to conceive and believed that past use of the pill was to blame. The pharmaceutical companies and doctors will tell you that the pill doesn't do that, but I have lived long enough to know that medical science is not omniscient. Not so many years ago it was common knowledge that X-rays had no harmful side effects. Besides, these (or rather, some of these) are the people who call abortion safe and legal.

We've heard a lot of challenges on this topic over the years. Here are some of the questions and our answers.

Q: Don't you think God wants us to use common sense in family planning?

A: No, I think He wants us to use good sense, which is not common. It's not good sense to violate Scripture or to make major decisions without studying the Bible for principles and commands. I believe that the issue of human life is not under man's domain except where explicitly stated in Scripture, for example in cases of self-defense, capital punishment and war.

Q: Isn't it irresponsible to take on financial obligations you may not be able to meet?

A: Yes. But that's a matter to be decided before marriage. God sent His Son to a woman engaged to a man who was a carpenter, that is he already had a trade established before taking on a family. Besides, you may have only one child and find him or her to cost you tens of thousands in unexpected medical or other costs. Only God knows the future, but the Psalmist knew the past. He wrote in Psalm 37:25,

I have been young, and now I am old;
Yet I have not seen the righteous forsaken,
Or his descendants begging bread.

Besides the fact that we have God's promise to feed us (without reference to family size) I think most people could be much more productive than they are and reap higher incomes by so doing. If you are stuck in the rut of thinking in terms of 40-hour weeks and consistent paychecks I suggest you do some sniffing around for opportunities. As I've told you, I had terribly insufficient income for years. It was not until God got me to a certain point in learning diligence and creativity that we began to get the ends to meet. I found the biographies of Ben Franklin, Sam Walton and Col. Sanders a big help in broadening my thinking. I also suggest you stay entirely out of debt and beware of sneaky self-indulgence.

Q: How can I give adequate attention to my children if I have ten instead of two?

A: Congratulations on a responsible question. We have found that we certainly can't spend the time with our youngest child, baby Tucker Sean that we spent with Rickey at the same age. But Tuck has many more people to pay attention to him. Everybody loves him and the younger girls even fight over who gets to hold him. As I write this it was just last night that Marilyn couldn't get Tuck to go back to sleep after waking up around 3 AM. She finally took him downstairs and gave him to Rick. When I got up this morning I found Rick asleep on the sofa with Tuck asleep on his chest.

We have also found that lots of hugs help. Physical contact seems to go a long way in making a child feel special. Another idea is our "special nights" when Marilyn and I take one child out to supper at a restaurant and try to give him or her our undivided attention for a while.

Q: If I use contraception, won't God overrule it and give me a child if He really wants me to have one?

A: I heard a Christian college professor express that very viewpoint when I was a newlywed. I don't agree, however. If you take action to cut off your fertility, God may or may not act to reverse the consequences. The same applies if you take action to cut off your head.

To me, it seems that this question gets the issue backward. Why not let God plan your family as He did for people in Scripture? Let Him open and close the womb as He knows best rather than doing something questionable and expecting Him to overrule your mistakes.

Q: I'm going bonkers with the three children I have now. How could I manage more?

A: To make a specific suggestion, I'd have to know why you can't manage your three. It could be that you need to learn to discipline your children. It could be that you need your husband to be more involved. It could be that you need to learn some techniques of household management. Denying God the future Christian servants He wants is not the answer. Find a mom who does things well and learn how she does it. Do some research on housecleaning and home management at the library. Think about it, pray about it, discern the root problems and attack them one at a time. If your house is not in order, you already have problems. Problems won't start with additional children.

Q: What about adding to the overpopulation problem?

A: I don't believe there is an overpopulation problem. I think we have a stewardship problem. The world is still a comparatively empty place and modern technology is doing a good job of keeping up with increasing needs. I believe that it's those who hate babies who are propagating the myth of a crowded planet. Read *The Birth Dearth* by Ben Wattenberg for more information.

Q: What about the Christian woman who wants a career, perhaps in a full-time ministry? Won't motherhood limit her freedom to make a contribution to the cause of Christ?

A: Ask Susannah Wesley.

Q: I wouldn't mind having more children but my wife doesn't want any more. Shouldn't I honor her wishes?

A: Again, I don't feel that life prevention is something we humans have the authority to practice. In the extremely rare case of a woman who would certainly die if she tried to complete a pregnancy, thoughtful people could make a good argument either way. One could say that the mother's life is as important as a life not yet conceived. Another could say that God is the God of the impossible and we should let Him decide life and death issues. I have an opinion on the subject which I believe is Scriptural but I'm not going to tell you because I think there's another issue that is a much more common problem.

Why doesn't your wife want more children? Are your children rebellious? If so, get to work and discipline them. Is your wife under financial pressure? If so, discern where the problem lies (get some wise counsel). If the problem is lack of diligence or responsibility on your part, limiting your family size won't help much. Did your wife suffer from intrusive medical procedures during childbirth? You may need to find different obstetric care.

In a nutshell, I'd say if your wife doesn't want more children the first thing to do is question whether God is using that as a cue to some responsibility of yours. Don't let excuses masquerade as reasons.

One faithful child of God can be a powerful weapon of righteousness. But two are twice as many as one. And three are better still.

It's been calculated that if each of my twelve children has twelve children and so does each of my grandchildren and so on for five generations, that in the fifth generation my descendants and their spouses will number 271,000 people. That's a lot of prayers, a lot of letters to the editor, a lot of calls to congressmen. It's a lot of influence in many, many ways.

The great preacher of colonial days, Jonathan Edwards is one of my favorite examples of the potential of a large Christian family. I took this excerpt from one of my children's history books:

Through his keen theological and philosophical study, his clear preaching of the Gospel and his profound writing, Jonathan Edwards contributed greatly to the Great Awakening...

Over a much longer period of time, Edwards contributed much to America's spiritual heritage, not only through the long-lasting effects of his preaching but also through his posterity. He left behind him thirteen

godly children who produced a long line of outstanding American citizens, including fourteen college presidents (Ed. note: This was back in the days when American colleges were training schools for preachers rather than citadels of humanism), **one hundred college professors; one hundred pastors, missionaries and Bible teachers; sixty doctors; over one hundred lawyers and judges; and sixty authors and editors. In 1900 Edwards was elected to the American Hall of Fame.**

Children are blessings, God says so. I'm satisfied He is a better family planner than I am.

Yes, They're All Ours

FAMILY SNAPSHOTS
Part VIII

Little Rickey was a bundle of energy and creativity. He came up with some of the most off-the-wall stuff.

He was about three when we were working out in fthe garden, preparing it for planting. I went into the house for a minute and came back out to find little Rickey chopping away frantically (as he did everything) with a hoe at the edge of the garden. Chopchopchopchopchopchop.
I walked over to him.
"How's it going, Rickey?"
He looked up for a split second. Chopchopchopchop chopchopchop. Then he shouted as he always did when doing something active,
"I'M PLANTING SOUP !!!" Chopchopchopchopchop.

One snowy day Marilyn glanced out the window where little Rickey was playing. Just as she looked she saw the snowman fall over. In came Rickey, out of breath and excited as usual. And as usual, shouting.
"MOMMY! MOMMY! THE SNOWMAN FELL OVER!!
"Really, Rickey? Why did he fall over?""
"BECAUSE I WAS CLIMBING ON HIM!!"
"Why were you climbing on him, Rickey?"
"I WAS PUTTING EYE SHADOW ON HIM!!"

Chapter 9

SAVOR THE SEASONS

If anybody ever invents a time machine, I want the first one off the assembly line. I'll have a thousand things I want to do. I'll explore history and find out what really happened on a number of occasions. I'll return to my childhood and try to make peace with some of the painful things that happened to me and revisit the happy times at Grandad's farm with my cousins. But the first, the very first thing I'll do, is go back to when my children were little.

Oh, what I'd give to see my big boys small again. I used to get bored sometimes with pulling them in the wagon or pushing them on the swings but I'd give a lot to be able to do it again. I don't think I could ever tire of it. To be able to carry them on my shoulders again, to tickle them until they screamed. To have nobody around who knew that Dad wasn't perfect, that is except Mom. To be able to hug and kiss my boys without embarrassing them.

Back in my beloved house painting days I was working on a big house for an elderly lady who was a true gentlewoman. It was the summer of 1979 and it was hot. Not because it was 1979, but because it was summer. Marilyn had dropped by on her way home from her prenatal visit to the doctor. I climbed down off my ladder and walked across the yard to hear the news. Marilyn was due to deliver soon and I wondered what the doctor had said.

"He said I'd better hurry up and get home," she told me. "Said it could come any time."

We were planning on our second home birth. Marilyn had been treated so callously at Virginia Baptist Hospital when Tim was born that I swore I'd never take her there to give birth again. So we had had Nathan at home, much to the shock of our neighbor, Sandy across the street. I wish I'd had my camera ready. I'd gotten several pictures of Nate very early in his life but I'd sure have saved film for a shot of Sandy's face when Marilyn first threw the covers back if I'd known what her reaction was going to be like.

When Marilyn drove away she agreed to call me immediately if she had any strange sensations before my regular time to arrive home. I saw Mrs. Holt, my customer a few minutes later. When I told her it looked as if the new one would be along soon, she smiled.

"You're a rich man, Mr. Boyer," she said warmly.

And I was. And I am. But it's striking how often I forget and have to be reminded that I really am wealthy. Sometimes I feel sort of poor. I've long suspected that whoever said that the best things in life are free never paid an obstetrician's bill.

As we planned this book one thing we hoped to accomplish was to give some encouragement to young parents who are now going through seasons we've already passed. Looking back on our marriage we see so many times when we wanted to know why the pressure was on us and whether it would ever end. It would be very gratifying to think that those trials were partly for the purpose of preparing us to share hope with those who come behind us.

As I write this I have a couple of couples in mind. I know one young family with two small children who are having second thoughts about letting God plan their family because of the stresses they're undergoing with the little ones they have now. Another young couple we know have one baby and feel that their hands (and possibly their quiver) might be just about full what with the demands of parenting and paying the bills without a well-established income. Both these couples talk to us about their pressures almost apologetically as if they feel that we're going to look down disdainful noses at them.

But that's very far from the case. If they only knew how we'd like to be with them in the middle of some sleepless night, to give them a hug and tell them about the times we've walked the floor with sick or restless little people. And to assure them that this won't last forever.

We see the past through rose-colored glasses to some extent, but still we have a pretty good memory of how it was. The future we see as through a glass darkly, but we have our experience to give us some idea what it will probably be like. It's usually the present, or at least some features of it, that is hardest to focus in and examine.

When I was a boy my cousins, brothers and myself used to swim in Grandad's muddy pond in the back pasture. There were cows in that pasture and the pond was their watering hole. It sickens me to think of swimming in that water now, but you know how boys are. We loved it and that smelly mud just served as something to soften the pond bottom and as ammunition to throw at each other.

But one thing we couldn't do in that muddy water was see anything. Once I was swimming under the water trying to sneak up on somebody when my hand struck another hand in the mud of the bottom. Aha. Somebody was trying to sneak up on me at the same time. I grabbed the hand and gave a jerk, hoping to startle whoever was on the other end of it, maybe even assist him in swallowing a little water. But the hand wasn't attached to anything.

I panicked. I managed to get my feet under me and scramble to a standing position in the waist-deep water. I had just enough breath left in me to give a terrified shriek as I threw the hand halfway across the pond. It was a frog.

The boys all laughed at me just as you're laughing now, shame on you. But you would have thought it was a severed hand too, if you'd seen as many scary movies as I had.

Visibility in the agitated water of a farm pond is not good. So it is with some of the stressful situations of family life. When you're outside the pond you can tell a lot about it and you can see plainly that it's not all that far across. But when you're the one swimming underwater in the middle of it all you know is that you're getting very short of breath.

One of my favorite passages of Scripture is Ecclesiastes 3:1-8. It's a good reminder that good times and bad times come and go and that we need to be prepared to experience some of each. In honor of those in the trenches of parenthood and especially those younger than my wife and myself, I'd like to offer the following thoughts on this passage as it might apply in the lives of parents.

Ecclesiastes 3, verse 1: **To every *thing there is* a season, and a time to every purpose under the heaven:**

God connects times with purposes. He doesn't promise to tell us what the purpose is while we're in the time, and He may not tell us before we enter Heaven. But remember in the tough seasons and the peaceful times as well that God has His purposes. Especially in the season of pressure, use only so much energy trying to discern God's reasons; He may not want you to know them yet. Learn to rest in the fact that your Father never wastes suffering.

Verse 2a: **A time to be born, and a time to die;**

You were a newborn yourself and it wasn't so long ago. The time will come when you will be called away from this planet. Between those two times, there are many seasons.

The one you're in will end and another will begin. Remember that your life has both a beginning and an end and let that humble and motivate you. Your children are your bequest to the needy world you will be leaving.

Verse 2b: **a time to plant, and a time to pluck up** *that which is* **planted;**

There are times to sow good seed in the hearts of your children. The time you spend reading his or her favorite Bible story for the umpteenth time isn't wasted. There is also a time for pulling weeds. Be alert to pluck up unworthy attitudes or false philosophies the enemy tries to sow in your wheat.

Verse 3a: **A time to kill, and a time to heal;**

My first dog had to be put to sleep because he was very sick. I was only a small boy and in bed with measles when my father gave Sport the pills hidden in some meat. His end was peaceful which made it a little easier for me. It must have been hard on my dad, knowing how attached I was to my little dog. But he had the call to make. He was Dad. There were times when pets were nursed back to health too, and the day when Dad carried me into the emergency room with burns from firecracker powder on my face. Parents help with healing, too.

Verse 3b: **a time to break down, and a time to build up;**

There are seasons of correction when an attitude or habit has to be broken down by discipline. There are times when a little person has experienced disappointment, rejection or

131

failure and needs to be built up. Time for the rod and time for a hug.

Verse 4: **A time to weep, and a time to laugh, a time to mourn and a time to dance;**

There was a time to weep when my Grandad died and I couldn't afford to go home to be with the family. At other times I've cried when I felt I had failed as a parent. There's been a lot of laughter too, at the goofiness of a teenage clown or the antics of a toddler.

There is a time to grieve over the loss of a little one who died before birth or surprisingly soon thereafter. There is also a time to rejoice in a healthy birth or celebrate the acquisition of a fine son- or daughter-in-law.

Verse 5a: **A time to cast away stones, and a time to gather stones together;**

At times I've thrown rocks out of the yard into the garden so I could run the lawn mower and then thrown what I was sure were identical rocks out of the garden into the yard so I could run the tiller. Occasionally some rocks have been gathered up with other junk and hauled to the dump. I've sometimes been guilty of casting away stones when I would have been wiser to gather them together. The little foibles of maintaining a home are part of the season.

Verse 5b: **a time to embrace, and a time to refrain from embracing;**

Guiding your child in relationships with others is an important job that spans many seasons. Many temptations come through companionship and decisions as to whom to embrace and whom to avoid are critical. The day comes in fact when a choice of a life partner has to be made and committed to. It's a season for parents to stand firm and families to stand together in supporting the new couple for life.

Verse 6a: **A time to get, and a time to lose; a time to keep, and a time to cast away;**

We have some gains, we have some losses. Some things are worth the time and effort to acquire and own, other things only distract from our purposes with their demand for maintenance and protection. Blessed is the parent whose life is uncluttered with excess possessions so he has time to enjoy his family undistracted.

Verse 7a: **A time to rend, and a time to sew;**

There is a time to repair a damaged garment and a time to throw one away and go shopping for a replacement. Some clothes, like some associations, aren't worth repairing because they never really fit properly anyway.

Verse 7b: **a time to keep silence, and a time to speak;**

From time to time a parent has to bite his tongue and let a little person learn from his own mistakes. On the other hand there are those times when a warning or instruction or rebuke is just what the doctor ordered. Blessed is that parent who has the discernment to know the difference.

Verse 8a: **A time to love, and a time to hate;**

Parents know what it is to love, to have one's heartstrings so entwined with the woven strands of a loved one's life experiences that the other's joy and pain are his own as well. Because they know the holding power of love they yearn to teach their children to love that which is of God in the world and hate that which is wrong or unworthy. We love Him because He first loved us. The fear of the Lord is to *hate* evil.

Verse 8b: a time of war, a time of peace.

So much of our life is a battle. But the war is won and some day the last skirmishes will end and peace will settle over the landscape. We have battles, especially spiritual battles, for our children and our grandchildren. But the lulls between fights are the seasons of peace we need to rebuild our strength. As we look forward to the lasting peace at the end of the campaign, let's remember that the exertions of the battle will be rewarded.

The next few lines of Ecclesiastes 3 are a fitting conclusion to these thoughts:

Verses 9-11a: What profit hath he that worketh in that wherein he laboureth? I have seen the travail, which God hath given to the sons of men to be exercised in it. He hath made everthing beautiful in his time...

And parenthood, though labor, is beautiful.

In the early days of our parenthood it sometimes seemed that life would go on forever as it was going then. We'd never have any money, we'd never have a child old enough to babysit, we'd never have air conditioning. I was so tense as a

134

young man that I made life harder for myself and those around me.

I've heard Marilyn say that when she had three children life was tougher than it was with eight because when she had only three there were no big helpers. Two were in diapers and Rickey was a bundle of energy. Now of course we have some good help trained and that is a blessing but the extra needs in the family are felt, too. It takes a tremendous expenditure of time, finances and effort to do what we do.

But by now we know that it won't always be this way. There may be tougher times with a sick child or persecution such as when we were in court over home education. And there will almost certainly be easier times too, when more of our children are mature teens and ready to carry their own weight and somebody else's, too. All we know for sure is that everything that comes to pass, passes.

One of the blessings of our hard seasons is the powerful motivation they have been to train our children in wisdom. Not infrequently I find myself telling one or more of my children, "Now don't be like me and do what I did when I ___ " And fill in the blank. There are those who say that kids have to make all their own mistakes. I say baloney. We all agree that it's not a good idea to stand in the path of a speeding truck and we didn't learn it by experience. Some things have to be learned by one's own mistakes but a lot of things can be learned from the experiences of others. I want my children to learn from my mistakes and not have to make their own. I have enough mistakes in my repertoire to go around.

Some of the things I've learned through bitter experience and which I want to pass on to my children would include these:

Stay in the Word.

Work hard even when you're discouraged. It helps.

Guard your heart from sin and distraction as well.

Consider self-employment. There's flexibility when it's done right.

Develop a personal and family ministry. If others aren't ministering, don't complain; minister instead.

Keep a screwdriver handy. There are loose doorknobs everywhere.

One day in the fall when Rick and Tim were little guys around kindergarten age we went to the woods to give our dogs a run. I kept the dogs in the car at first and sent the boys running off through the trees to hide so the dogs could track them down. I watched them trot eagerly away in their jackets and sneakers while a shower of yellow and orange leaves cascaded down through the clear autumn air. The thought struck me that this was a good day in my life and that I should enjoy it. Those were my precious little sons galloping away through the leaves and they were healthy and happy. They had a wonderful mother and two baby brothers and dogs to play with in the woods. It was a good day in their lives as well as mine.

It's a shame that it seems so easy to get distracted by a little difficulty from great blessings. The season in which we find ourselves is never all good or all bad but it is temporary and we should savor it while it's here. I was reminiscing a while back with a man I see only once or twice a year. His son was my best friend in junior high and high school and they put up with seeing a lot of me. As I reminded him of some of the things we used to do together he said, "Yes, those were good years."

They hadn't seemed so good to me because it was during those years that my family was going through some hard times and I was struggling to live with myself while growing

136

up. But talking to him reminded me that there had been some wonderful times and dear friends. I'm glad those years look good to him in memory because he made them better for me.

One day in May Marilyn was sitting out in a lawn chair during a rare moment of leisure and watching the children play in the yard. She said the strongest feeling came over her that God was saying to her, "Enjoy this day. This is a precious time with your children. Treasure this day in your heart."

That's something I've had a hard time learning and it's earned me a few wifely scoldings. I don't know why contentment has been such a hard lesson to learn but it must be one of my besetting sins. I'd never make a guru because I can't sit still. But I'm getting better.

Fortunately there is enough nostalgia in my makeup to compensate for mental hyperactivity. I love to sit and look at our photos. The children love it too, and we have some pretty tattered photo albums. There ought to be a custom that every couple receives a VCR for a wedding present. All we had to start with was a cheap instamatic but I'm glad we had it. Still, I do wish we'd had a VCR or movie camera to watch baby's first steps and early attempts at swimming. And about a million other things. Besides my own memories, I think there's a lot of value in building memories for the children to take with them into adulthood and families of their own.

The burdens of young parents are keenly felt and it's often hard to drop a chore in the middle and run for the camera. But it's very rewarding if you can just get used to the idea that the housework will keep while you snap a picture or two. I would never encourage you to be a sloppy housekeeper but there are priorities. If you're not enjoying your children then you're too busy. Children will grow up overnight whether you want them to or not and you can't afford to miss little happenings that will one day be your memories.

If you're like me you can think of a million things you'd like to have time to do. Worthwhile things, too. I'd like to learn to play a musical instrument, be more involved in politics, be more active in my church and read a lot of good books. Some of which have been on my shelf for years. Many times I've thought how I could improve myself if I only had time. But God reminds me that He is improving me through the very common responsibilities that I think are keeping me from my chosen pursuits.

God knows us better than we know ourselves. He knows what challenges, responsibilities and opportunities to bring into our lives as He builds a life curriculum for each of us. It is when we kick against the pricks and are constantly looking for something else more fulfilling to do that we miss fulfillment. In my single days I never would have suspected that rinsing dirty diapers in the toilet was the least bit enlightening or noble. Yet now when I hear someone preach on faith or endurance and I suspect he's never been on his knees before the porcelain throne, I can't help wondering whether he really has authority to speak.

I heard a story about an elderly preacher and his wife who went to hear a promising young preacher speak to a large and responsive crowd. As they walked home afterward the lady said, "My, wasn't that young man a great preacher!"

To which her husband replied, "Yes, after he has suffered for a while, he will be a great preacher."

I guess most of us don't think of having a baby barf down one's shoulder as suffering for the Lord, but in the final analysis what else could you call it?

I used to think that I was wasting my potential by not being in a full-time ministerial position. These days I'm coming to see that there's no more important ministry than the stewardship of little lives. We moms and dads hold the keys to future generations. We mustn't get bogged down in the daily grind and forget to smell the roses on the one hand and revel in the prospect of future achievement on the other.

This business of being in the ministry seems to apply to women as well as men. I've known guys who put their families through torture trying to finish college and get that paper in their hand. But for every one of them I suspect I've known at least one woman who was itching for more of a ministry as well. We have lady friends who seem always on the lookout for a friend or neighbor who is an emotional basket case so they can minister. We know other women who express the desire to "leave their mark on the world." Do you think Susannah Wesley left her mark on the world?

It's interesting that the moms who are looking for a ministry outside their families often pick people who never seem to make spiritual progress. Maybe they lack the spiritual discernment to refrain from casting pearls before swine or maybe they naturally gravitate to people who have promise of being a long-term market for their own misplaced mother instincts. It's also worth remarking that I've observed women diligently but fruitlessly ministering to other women when their own husbands and children have unmet needs. Where is their authority to speak?

The principle in Scripture is for older women to teach younger women to love their husbands, love their children, be sensible, pure, workers at home, kind, and subject to their own husbands (see Titus 2 NASV). Now I would think that the first requirement to teach pottery would be the ability to make a pot. I would also think it logical that the first requirement to teach all these womanly skills to others would be the demonstration of them in one's own family.

God seems to be serious about the principle of seasons. Note that He wants older women teaching younger women. He also gives a list of curriculum components. It seems that younger women should concentrate on learning to do their job in their own family before aspiring to teach others. It's more glamorous teaching a ladies' Bible study than dipping diapers but evidently they both have their season.

There will be different seasons in the lives of your children, we've found. There was a time when we were living in our little yellow house in Concord and had two, then three then four little boys. I was young and eager, wanting to get into full-time ministry work and leaving no stone unturned looking for God's big opportunity for me. I was eager to get into the Lord's work and out of painting. My wife stuck close to her home and children while my eyes were on the ends of the earth. In the long run it was not my eagerness but my children that gave me an opportunity to speak.

Marilyn was so faithful in training her children. She had those little guys memorizing Scripture and character qualities and learning responsibility in the family. We dreamed of the day when they would take their places in the adult world and we could enjoy the fruits of our labors in their success. It seemed a long time that they were just little kids whom people thought very bright, but who were too young to really accomplish anything.

Then one day we woke up and our little boys were doing adult things. We had sons ushering in church, playing the the piano, singing in the choir, remodeling the nursery. They were going to political conventions and working the polls. They were helping me make a living for their siblings and building a reputation in the community for responsibility and diligence. Gone was our secluded life at Concord which could have been even more happy and peaceful if only I had known how to wait on God and savor the season.

It was no coincidence that as my children grew so did our outreach. The larger our family became and the more our children began to do, the more people were interested in what Marilyn and I were learning. I had thought as a young man that I had so much to say and that the world was suffering because there was no platform from which I could say it. Frankly that embarrasses me now because I'm finding that there is more I don't know with every year that passes. And as I grow dumber my children advance in their roles in the world outside the walls of our home and we, their parents get more and more respect.

It's a mistake to try to make our children grow up too fast. I always looked forward to the days when our kids would be teenagers and now I wonder how I could have forgotten so quickly what it was like to be a teenager. I should have spent those early seasons enjoying my children as little ones and making the most of each day with them. Some people fear making their children too dependent on Mommy and Daddy. That's like being afraid of gravity. Gravity has some disadvantages, but nothing to compare to being flung into outer space if gravity suddenly ceased to exist. I hope my children always feel the tug of home. I see the results of the opposite condition all through our society and wonder if all those working mothers and career-oriented, status-conscious dads really think it's worth it to miss out on the springtime of their children's lives.

If Marilyn and I could offer some suggestions to younger parents we would tell them to look at the bright side of each season of life rather than longing for a season that is not yet due or is gone and can't return. We lived through a time when we had no big boys to babysit while we went out together and that seemed a disadvantage. Now we know that it was much easier having a quiet household than it is now. We could get everybody in bed at the same time at night and Marilyn could even get some quiet time during afternoon naps. We have our babysitters now but brother, do we need them. Gone are the long, quiet evenings at home with lots of time to talk. Now we have to go out to dinner to discuss anything at length. It's not that our children are terribly unruly, but fourteen people in the same house can distract each other.

It may be that our twilight years will be our best. Then we'll have our children raised and the financial burden eased so that we can rest and play more. I never want to retire, but I'd like to have more choice in how I spend my time. I want to spend it fishing with my children and grandchildren. I want to bask in the glow of sons and daughters who are honoring God and enjoy getting acquainted with my new children by marriage. I want to see the family network expand and influence the world around us for the Lord. I'd like to write a book now and then and occasionally have opportunity to speak to parent groups, encouraging them to make the most of the seasons of their children's lives.

One thing I don't want in my later years is to regret my earlier life. I don't want to look back on the times when there were little ones constantly wanting to be read to or played with in the sandbox and think that I never quite had enough time for those things. By then I'll know so very well that children don't continue to want those things forever. I hope I'll look back and remember thankfully that I subordinated my own interests and made the effort to invest in theirs.

I've already lived long enough to know that this season will pass. Today life is demanding. We have infants to care for at the same time we have young men needing our help in making the transition into the adult world. We face constantly changing needs, clothing is continually being outgrown and it seems there is no end to the errands needing to be run. But it wasn't always this way and it won't always be this way. Everything that comes to pass, passes.

When the next season comes I hope I look back on this one and recall that I wrung the good out of every day and took the lumps with some degree of patience. I hope that my children will remember happily how I dealt with them and want to deal with their children the same way. Lord, teach us to number our days that we may apply our hearts unto wisdom.

FAMILY SNAPSHOTS
Part IX

One Sunday night we came home late from church. Marilyn and I were tired as we always were late on Sunday evenings.

Four-year-old Rickey wanted to know what was for supper. That, of course inspired three-year-old Tim.

"Yeah, what's for supper?" he echoed his brother.

I tried to convince them they weren't really hungry and that we'd all better just forget supper and go to bed. But it didn't work. They were not to be denied.

I did a little scouting.

"I don't see much, boys," I said discouragingly, my head deep in the interior of the refrigerator. "Don't you think maybe this time we should just..."

"I'm hungry," moaned little Rickey.

"Me, too," chimed in Tim.

This would never do. There was nothing in here that would be quick to cook. Just odds and ends of leftovers. The is called for some creativity.

"Oh, wow boys!!" I exclaimed. "Look what we can have!"

"What? What is it?" Rickey crowded close to the refrigerator.

"What is it?" copied Tim, warming up.

"We can have bean pie and corn pizza! Oh, all right! Oh, boy, this'll be great! Bean pie and corn pizza! Wow!"

Of course the boys were excited by now. They both looked up eagerly as I emerged from the refrigerator with bowls of cold corn and beans.

"Tell you what, guys. You sit up at the table and I'll have this ready in just a second. This'll be fantastic! It's not every day you get bean pie and corn pizza!"

Almost breathlessly they watched as I warmed up the cold vegetables and then spooned them onto slices of bread on their plates. I set the plates in front of them and handed them each a fork.

"Look at that, guys! Bean pie and corn pizza! It's not every day you get to eat stuff like that!" Which was true.

Marilyn had heard snatches of the conversation as she put baby Nathan to bed and now she entered the kitchen and watched wide-eyed as the boys emptied their plates.

They finished the last morsels, kissed Mommy and Dadddy and headed off to bed, content at having a special treat as a climax to their day.

"You really have some bright ideas, don't you?" my wife said wonderingly. "Bean pie and corn pizza."

I was back inside the refrigerator.

"Got anything in here that's fit to eat?"

Chapter 10

THE RAISING AND/OR TRAINING OF HUMANS

I've been told that you don't 'raise' children, you 'raise' corn. The proper term in reference to bringing up children is 'rearing' them. Child rearing, you see. I've never been crazy about the term 'rearing' because I didn't grow up with it and it makes me think of what you occasionally have to do to a child's 'rear' in order to 'raise' him right.

It's interesting to reflect on the various approaches to child training. I've met people who said that you have to reason with children, help them see that they're making bad choices when they disobey. On the other end of the spectrum, I can recall my mother telling how when one of the children in her family earned a spanking the rest of the kids got one as well. I guess her father figured that there's usually collaboration, so why miss a likely cohort.

As a matter of fact this early apprenticeship made a pretty good disciplinarian out of Mom. I remember doing a little science experiment once that ended up setting the stuff in the kitchen trash can on fire. It's amazing how much heat a little flame can generate.

We have found that discipline is a balancing act. We've seen parents who have no control over their children because they never hold them accountable for their behavior and we've seen parents who seem to spank for every little infraction as if that were the only form of correction that works. The Scripture says he that spareth the rod hateth his son, but that is only one small part of the training of children.

In this chapter we won't talk all that much about correction because we have observed over the years that

146

correction is being dealt with in a number of recent books that have met with fairly wide acceptance. Those books are important not only because the topic is essential but also because of the false teachings that have gone forth about how children are innately good and spanking is violence, etc. But now that others have dealt with the correction end of child training we hope to address the instruction aspect.

The reason we titled this chapter as we did is to indicate that there is a difference between raising and training. In common parlance raising means producing young and caring for their needs so that they grow up healthy, such as in raising rabbits. Training refers to inculcating patterns of behavior, as in training dogs to fetch or herd or track. I suppose in reference to children the word 'rearing' is intended to indicate both but I still don't like it and I'm not going to use it, so there. After all, this is my book.

In the business of bringing up children, the Christian parent wants to go farther than having an orderly home and children whose behavior is correct. He wants to build godly character in his children so that when they leave home and the threat of punishment no longer looms over their heads they will still do right outwardly because they are right inwardly. Wise moms and dads realize that success and joy in life come from within and outward achievement brings only limited satisfaction if one's heart isn't right.

It is sad but true that parents are by and large not receiving much instruction in how to be parents. Although it has seen a tremendous resurgence in the last twenty years, the emphasis on family life in American Christianity is not what it should be. There are a number of popular books out on the subject but the topic is still not getting the emphasis it deserves in the local churches. What's more, much of the teaching one hears on the topic is flawed because of the education of the writers. Scriptural principle is intermingled with humanistic psychology.

When people ask me about how to learn to be good parents I advise them to find some good parents and pick their brains. That, after all is how you'd go about learning to be a good golfer or any one of a number of other callings. And to find good parents, I tell them, don't go to parents who think they know a lot. Go rather to parents who don't think they are all that wonderful but whose children demonstrate their parents' success. Those parents are the ones who have something to teach you, and especially if they have successful teenage or adult children.

Marilyn and I are not perfect parents. We're not perfect anything. This chapter is not to impart the child training secrets of the world's greatest mom and dad but to share some of the lessons we've learned through the years as we've worked our way through the various challenges of parenthood.

In Scripture there is a plan given for education. It is called discipleship and it is a far cry from what modern man calls education, which is schooling. Discipleship is a relationship, schooling is institutionalization. We have come to believe that child training in the family is the purest form of discipleship.

It seems to Marilyn and me that the process of bringing up children is a matter of taking them by the hand and walking with them through life. This is what Jesus did with His disciples. He had them involved in the work from the beginning to the extent that they were able, with increasing responsibility to correspond to increasing ability. At the same time, He was having occasional lecture and discussion sessions with them.

We view the family as a team much like the twelve disciples. As the children grow their abilities increase and we give them more responsibility, doing our best to make the amount of responsibility appropriate. At the same time, we're teaching them the principles and information we think they should know about this business of living.

We don't view ourselves as zoo keepers, responsible only for the health and security of our charges. Neither do we consider ourselves prison guards, concerned only about containment and control. Nor are we trainers, working to get the children to exhibit certain outward behaviors on cue like trained porpoises. Our plan is to do what we are called to do in life and take our children along with us in the doing of it to ever increasing degrees. At the same time as we involve them in the doing we are trying to teach them the knowledge and attitudes they will need for success when they are no longer under our direct care. We feel that both the exhortation and the experience are needed.

Marilyn and I created an interesting combination of parenting philosophies when we got married. She, being oriented toward a career in classroom education, was very much into academic teaching. My teaching experience was with police dogs and I was interested in motivation and behavior. Especially obedient behavior.

Both of our philosophies were very incomplete of course; we knew very little of child training. Fortunately, when our first child arrived he wasn't ready for much training. He spent most of his time sleeping, yelling or smelling bad. But Marilyn was not one to neglect his education until it might be too late and so she came up with an impressive variety of teaching tools she was sure would make a child prodigy out of him in short order.

She filled his crib with stuffed toys, rattles and unidentifiable gizmos to stimulate his interest. She hung a wind-up mobile above his head so that he would have moving objects to watch. She could carry him around the house and introduce him to the different attractions of the home. "Look, Rickey, window! See window, Rickey?" It got to be a bit much when riding in the car. "Look, Rickey, tree! See tree? Oh, looky there! Truck, Rickey, Truck! Ooh, BIG truck, Rickey!" He was only a few months old but I guess the drooling was an expression of enthusiasm.

Larry Coy's Sunday school class changed Marilyn's focus. Larry taught us about the power of Scripture memorization and meditation. He also talked about the potential of ministering to a child's spirit instead of majoring on his mind. I liked that talk because of what the Bible had done for me since I had begun to get into it. And Marilyn could immediately see about a thousand ways to teach Scripture to her children.

Down came the alphabet charts from the nursery wall. Up went the Bible verses in Magic Marker on construction paper. Soon instead of showing Rickey all the points of interest such as curtains and refrigerators Marilyn was rocking him and having theological discussions.

As the other children came along and they all grew older Marilyn really got into her stride. I was beginning to have some input too, especially in teaching the boys to obey and introducing them to some basic wrestling techniques. And we were both learning.

One thing we're happy we came to understand early was that children want to please their parents even though that is in conflict with their natural willfulness. This realization helped us to concentrate on communicating our wishes clearly instead of working on enforcement to the extreme. We have known friends who seemed to feel that their children wouldn't obey unless they were spoken to in a harsh tone of voice, so that all directives were given in a scolding tone. This always made me uncomfortable because I knew from training dogs that if you gave a command in the same tone of voice in which you issued corrections, it was sometimes hard for the dog to understand whether he was being commanded or corrected and how to respond.

When we were in Florida I was contacted by a man about training his German Shepherd puppy for him. He had done some work with the dog he said, but he was limited in what he knew of obedience training. I went to his home to talk more about it.

The only scene I remember was the guy demonstrating how the puppy was learning to go in and out of the house on command. He came out of the house just fine. But when he was commanded to go back in he hit a snag. He was standing in the middle of the back yard and his master opened the storm door, stood against it to hold it open and commanded the pup to go inside. The dog took a step toward the door but hesitated. He wasn't disobeying, but it was clear that he was young, inexperienced and not entirely sure he understood the order correctly. If at this point the man had just repeated the command with a hand gesture and a couple of gentle words of encouragement, the puppy probably would have been reassured and trotted right in with a wag of the tail. But the fellow was not at all patient and he immediately became irate. He repeated the command louder and more roughly. This time I was sure the pup understood what was wanted but he knew his master was mad at him and was a bit hesitant to go right past him to enter the house. He whined and sat down on the grass. Of course his master really got irate then and totally ruined the training session by shouting at the dog some English expressions that even a German dog could understand.

The problem was not that the puppy didn't want to obey, nor after the first command at least, that he didn't understand what was wanted of him. But the anger of his master frightened him and he was afraid to pass within kicking distance to obey. I knew that man would have a lot of trouble training his dog because the dog didn't have confidence that he could please him. Had he been sure that if he tried to obey he would not be punished, he would have been an easy pup to work with because he was obviously paying attention.

Children can be discouraged too. They need to understand their parents' desires and have confidence that if they try to do right they will not be punished. Sadly, some parents are so impatient that they fly off the handle before the child has had a fair chance to comply.

In our early years we went through a period of time when we felt that our training wasn't being effective. One particular instance was when Marilyn went to the grocery store. This was in the years before we had built-in babysitters and she had to take all four of the little boys with her if I wasn't available to stay at home with them. Anybody who knows anything about marketing understands that the products for sale in any store are packaged and displayed so as to grab attention and arouse desire to purchase. A lot of the things in a supermarket are particularly attractive to children and my little guys were no exception. Marilyn felt that she was spending the whole time correcting the boys and rescuing stacks of cans instead of shopping. There was so much confusion involved that she felt that the boys were being very unmanageable. When she got home after one such pleasure excursion we talked about it.

As we discussed the situation we decided that we weren't faced with a case of mutiny, but that the boys just didn't know how to act in a supermarket. The only input they had received was in the form of being told what not to do after they had already done it. So I asked my wife what the boys should and shouldn't do in the store and we made some simple rules for them.

When we had the rules listed in words that the boys could undertand, we sat them down and explained the situation to them. There were some things to remember in the supermarket, we told them. They were to stay behind Mommy and the cart but within a few steps. They were to stay where Mommy could see them at all times. They were not to hang on the cart. They were to look with their eyes, not with their hands

After we had explained and repeated the rules a few times we made a training run to the store. Marilyn didn't need to buy a lot so we were able just to walk up and down the aisles and give most of our attention to the boys. They forgot the rules a few times but I reminded them and they began to get into the right pattern. From that day on Marilyn had very few problems in the supermarket. The boys knew the rules and only needed to be reminded now and then when some particularly intriguing item caught their attention and made them forget.

Since then we have used the training session idea in a number of different scenarios. Church is one such. Visiting in homes is another. The key is in keeping the rules few and simple so they're easy to remember and obey, then drilling the children on them before going into the store, home, church, car, restaurant or whatever the case is. It really works because most children would rather have their parents happy than fussing at them, and all they need is to have confidence that they know how to please Mom and Dad. There will always be a place for correction, but instruction must come first.

Most parents could greatly reduce their ulcer potential if they would just deal with issues of obedience in terms of before rather than after. Some people never seem to get around to giving their child any guidance until he's done something wrong. And he may not have even known in advance that it was wrong.

It seems that most people think of child training as a matter of reaction. That is, they seem to expect children to know instinctively what behavior is desired and if it is not forthcoming they get angry. Personally, I think a big part of the problem is that people are constantly distracted by entertainment. Oh, boy, you say, here goes Boyer on his soap box again. Well, you may get tired of my calling it to your attention but just the other day I was in the home of a neighbor and there were two televisions and a VCR all playing at the same time and within fifteen feet of each other. How can anyone living in such an environment ever have an original thought, let alone a creative one? Also very recently Marilyn and I talked to a school teacher who said that not only will her students' parents not turn off the television to help their children with their homework but they complain to the teacher that she assigns too much homework and doesn't leave the child enough time to watch TV. What has this society come to?

It takes more effort to train children in advance than to yell at them in arrears, but it makes for much less frustration.

This is all to make the first of two major points about which we feel strongly: It takes orderly effort to train children properly. It can't be done by accident and it can't be done by reaction. They have to be taught what is right behavior and right character and they need to see it exemplified in the lives of their parents.

Over the years we have tried to develop training projects whenever we identified character needs in our family just as we did with the grocery store affair. We've been around as a family longer now and it's not as often that we have to give advance instructions to the whole group. But still there are little ones coming along and occasionally we'll have a new experience for one of the little teammates.

The other main point I hoped to make in this chapter is that the physical environment of the home can be programmed to communicate character lessons to the family. We take this principle from Deuteronomy chapter 6. There we're told to write the words of God on the doorposts of our house and on our gates. Further, it instructs us to talk of them when we sit in our house, walk by the way, lie down and rise up. We're also to write them as a sign upon our hands and have them for frontlets for our foreheads. You get the impression God wants us to pay attention.

My smart little wife has found creative ways to put these ideas into practice. If you were to walk through our house you would see Scriptures on the border of the dining room wallpaper and on wall plaques throughout (doorposts and gates-physical structure), possibly verses on the tablecloth (for when you sit in your house), and maybe a child or two with a Scripture tee shirt (wearing apparel, like phylacteries and frontlets). In the children's bedrooms (for when they lie down and rise up) you would find Bible story window curtains, character quality quilts, even Bible theme wall hangings such as a stuffed cloth Noah's ark. I'm telling you, my wife is a sharp cookie.

And of course our room has some Bible motifs, too. We have plaques and things and until we redecorated we had pillow shams bearing Scriptures written to husbands and wives. For years we had a bedspread that Marilyn had lettered with verses from I Corinthians 13 (I facetiously suggested something from Song of Solomon but I'd never get up the nerve).

Marilyn has been creating these character building projects ever since our early days together and we finally got around to putting them in a book called *Hands-on Character*

155

Yes, They're All Ours

Building which lists her craft ideas, character games, obediences exercises and so forth, along with instructions for doing them and information as to where to order materials if needed (Forgive me for not sharing more about them here but I'm getting awfully tired of typing and besides I don't want to discourage you from buying another book. By the way, they make great Christmas gifts. Or for Mother's Day. Or Groundhog Day).

Besides giving our them active training and trying to build a Scripture-saturated home environment, we have found other influences that help our children to aspire to good character.

One of these influences is that of the heroes in their lives. I've mentioned this briefly before, but it's important enough to merit a second mention. You can tell an awful lot about a person if you can find out whom he admires. I never fail to get a sense of depression when as a guest in some home I see on a teenager's bedroom wall a poster showing one of those perverts who star in rock music. They're now even in Christian music, in case you live in a cave and haven't heard. I've seen posters of "Christian" rock stars who appear to be a mixture of lunatic, sixties hippy, transvestite and motorcycle thug. Marvelous role models for Christian young people.

Our children have possibly read more bographies than any other type of book. The lives of good people are an encouragement and inspiration. Think for a minute about the difference between a biography of Washington on a bedside table and a poster of a rock star on a bedroom wall. Where is there any comparison? Somebody ought to come out with a Christian Heroes poster series. Each poster could feature a big portrait of the hero or heroine and a couple of paragraphs about his or her life in small print at the bottom. I think it would be great to have George Whitefield, John Wesley, Robert E. Lee, Charles Finney, Corrie Ten Boom or

George Muller looking down on our children in their beds, daring them to greatness for God.

Another source of character encouragement for our children comes from the extended family. Your relatives may not even be Christians, but any character quality in their lives that you can praise to your children will make a contribution. As a matter of fact, it might serve as motivation for the relatives, too, to know that little eyes are turned toward them looking for an example.

I've also mentioned companions previously as an influence on character but they belong in this chapter. Besides, the influence of one's companions is so very powerful that it could be discussed at some length I think, without overkill. One of the reasons we educate our children at home is that we have the freedom to design a social environment for our children that is constructive rather than destructive. Marilyn and I have both been heard to comment that the idea of sending our children off to school where we have no control over who their companions are and how they act, is just totally foreign to us. We have the inestimable advantage of being able to limit our children's social contact with unhealthy companions and cultivate relationships with those who will help them be better people. We do most of our socializing as a family with other families. Marilyn and I seldom go out with another couple and the children seldom spend time with other children whose parents aren't present. Usually when we get together with another family it is a Christian family who shares similar goals with us.

If companionship were not critically important, why would the book of Proverbs alone contain sixty-some identifiable character types along with warnings to stay away from some? Solomon wrote Proverbs and since he was the the wisest man in the world he should be a pretty good authority on social life for young people. He gets no farther than fifteen verses into the book before saying, "My son, walk not thou in the way with them; refrain thy foot from their path..." And in fact the first warning concerning bad companions starts as early as verse ten of the first chapter. No company is better than bad company. But fortunately there is good company available for most of us.

These, then are some of the elements of character training that we have tried to build into the life of our family. I say again that children don't grow up to be good people by accident. Nor does training by reaction accomplish what the responsible parent wants. We have found that we can't be perfect parents and our children aren't perfect children. But after nineteen years of child 'raising' we are convinced that character grows best as does any other crop: In the right environment, on fertile soil and with careful cultivation.

FAMILY SNAPSHOTS
Part X

It was customary in our former church to have an informal testimony time in the last few minutes before dismissal of the service. One Sunday morning the pastor asked at the end of the sermon whether anyone had anything to share.

Five-year-old Rickey raised his hand. I wasn't surprised. The boy was far advanced for his age as I was sure all my children would be. He often had perceptive insights to share.

The pastor smiled and called on him. "Yes, Rickey?"

"I would like to share some Bible verses," Rickey said in his chattery, little boy voice. He gave the chapter and verse references and proceeded to rattle off such a string of Scriptures from memory that even I was impressed.

As my son finished the room was filled with the appropriate murmur of amazement and admiration. I basked in the glow of fatherly pride. One never knew when Rickey opened his mouth what would come out.

The pastor gave my son a smile as if to say that though he knew the little boy well, he was nonetheless constantly surprised at his early indications of intelligence, even brilliance.

"How old are you, Rickey?" he asked from the pulpit.

Evidently Rickey wanted to make sure the pastor could hear his reply from away up there, so he raised his voice and spoke loudly and clearly:

"JUST FIVE!"

As the house came down I looked around helplessly for a crack to trickle into.

After church a friend of mine sidled up to me and gave me a snide glance. Looking off in a direction away from me he murmured out the side of his mouth, "I'm just five and I'm real cute, see...."

One never knew when Rickey opened his mouth what was going to come out.

Chapter 11

LEAVING THE NEST

They say hindsight is always 20/20 but that's not true in my case. As I look back over my life I see some things that I did right and a lot of things I did wrong and in some cases I know now what I should have done differently. But that's in some cases, not all. In those cases where I can identify my mistakes, though, I'm determined to do whatever I can to help my sons and daughters avoid making the same ones.

I have now arrived at the point in life where I find myself faced with the prospect of watching some of my children leave my home and go about making their own way. This is one of those seasons when I could be tempted to wish that time had a stop button on it, as on an elevator. I could almost see my way clear to hit the button and stay forever between floors. But time waits for no dad and so I think a lot these days about what I'm doing to prepare my children for adult life.

I'm relieved to see that they aren't as eager to leave home as I was at their age. They feel at home at home (that's not a misprint) but I had chafed with impatience to get out from under the authorities of home and school. I wanted to be free of the things they made me do which bored and pressured me. I wanted to be free to do the things I liked to do: hang around with my friends, hunt, fish, ride horses and live on my farm. I wanted to be my own boss, make my own decisions and answer to nobody.

As the years of high school had crawled by my anticipation had grown. It's not that I didn't like school itself. All my friends were at school, I enjoyed the sports, I was having fun acting in the school plays, I liked the debate

161

and forensics contests. In fact about the only thing I didn't like about school was the school work. I saw no use at all in most of what they tried to teach us and the pressure of learning enough of it to forestall retribution kept me on edge at all times. I had learned to slide through the system with a minimum of effort, inerrantly sniffing out the path of least resistance. My attitude was the same at home, where a chore didn't have to run very fast to avoid being done by me.

My senior year was a picnic. I was a big shot now, one of the oldest class of students and looked up to by the younger kids. I was in the Lettermen's Club, was known for my acting and speaking prowess and had been voted "Wittiest Senior" for the yearbook. I had my first car and I used it. I had risen through the ranks socially and thought myself reasonably popular. I had arrived.

Up until my senior year when people began expecting me to make some career plans I had always assumed that I would be a farmer because a farmer is his own boss and can take time off to go fishing or hunting or swimming whenever he wants. That's what I thought. And he lives in the country where those things are accessible. But now it was pointed out to me by some bubble buster that farms cost money. Oh, yeah.

This complicated matters. I would have to get a job in order to earn money for the farm. Since an ordinary job such as working in a factory suggested discipline and boredom (both of which were anathema to me) that was not even a consideration. Casting about for an option that would combine income potential with enjoyable activity, I lit on the idea of being a high school drama teacher and wrestling coach. That seemed to fit perfectly because I loved theater and wrestling was my favorite sport. The drawback, of course was four more years of school work but others assured me that college was one long party with a maximum of social life and a minimum of study. I thought I could handle it.

Graduation night was in part a great experience. My classmates and I were the stars of the show. It was our night, the culmination of our dreams. My friends and I were seated alphabetically in long rows of folding chairs, slightly overwarm in our black caps and gowns as we listened to the speakers on the platform. Then we filed across to receive our diplomas and I forgot to move my tassel until I got back to my seat. In a few minutes it was over and the noise was deafening to those of us seated at floor level as the bleachers erupted with the applause of parents, relatives and friends of graduates.

To many of my classmates graduation meant the payoff for twelve years of diligent study. To some it was a stepping stone to a job. To others it was a milestone in an extended academic career. To me however, it meant that I was no longer a slave. I had not been in school by choice. I had not made more than a token effort toward academic achievement since the elementary grades. I can't remember ever seeing school as an opportunity; to me it was an obligation forced upon me. Now I was paroled. Now I was free.

But there was another feeling creeping in upon me that dampened my elation. Graduation meant the end of the world I had known. School was out for the last time and those two hundred people who had just graduated with me were the people who had been my classmates since first grade. The old structure had crumbled; many younger students remained who were good friends of mine but it would never be the same. My fellow graduates were separating for the last time and we wouldn't be seeing each other together again in the fall as always before. I didn't know it then but I was thoroughly peer dependent and I had developed a sense of identity that was rooted in school society. Earlier that evening I had been a comfortable member of the gang but with that roar of applause in the high school gym the gang had suddenly ceased to exist forever. I was happy and relieved that evening in May but as I walked to my car I couldn't quite escape a trace of sadness and a question I stifled for the present but which I knew I couldn't avoid forever: I wonder who I am now?

I loafed for the summer and left for college in the fall. But I had picked a small town community college and I found that out-of-town students didn't glide right into the social life. Everybody else had gone to high school across the street. I left at Christmas to enroll in a college a couple of hours from home in another direction but an obstacle as insignificant as a long registration line was enough to discourage me, so confused and unmotivated as I was at the time. I left in the afternoon and drove home to Mom's. My best friend was in college at Wichita State just across town from where we had grown up. He tried to persuade me to enroll there, assuring me that a number of our high school friends were now on campus. But I was still wandering in the never-never land of purposelessness. I could have penetrated the system and social structure at a new college but I had neither the motivation or the confidence to plunge in as a late registrant. I ended up going back to the community college fifty miles from home to avoid making a decision.

Surely somebody along the way must have tried to warn me that with freedom comes responsibility but it hadn't gotten through. I had been free to attend or not attend school for the past eight months and I still hadn't made a responsible decision about anything. I went back to college where I had started for little more reason than the anxiety of having to face getting and keeping a job.

I wouldn't have thought it possible, but life at the juco was even more boring than before. I lasted until the end of wrestling season but that was the limit of my endurance. When that last diversion was gone I dropped out even though it was the middle of the spring semester.

I had chosen the path of least resistance since graduation and it had led me to a dead end. I know now that I should have stayed home, worked a job, learned a trade and helped Mom, who still had two children to finish raising. But that was boring and required too much discipline, which means it was exactly what God knew I needed at the time.

It was a cruel joke on myself that I joined the military because I didn't have enough discipline for a full-time job. Within a few weeks after leaving the boredom and demands of college I was standing at parade rest on a drill field for hours at the mercy of a sergeant who made Attilla the Hun look like Ward Cleaver.

You know the rest of my story since then.

God rules and He overrules. My aimless wanderings to avoid responsibility had led me into the military, where for the first time I was given responsibilities I couldn't squirm out of. Looking back twenty years it all makes so much sense. The service gave me the discipline I had missed earlier in life, led me to my future bride and moved me to where I could find a church that would meet the needs I had at the time. It was through a letter that church received from a Christian college in Virginia that I was led to eventually move my young family to the place that would be our home for the next twenty years. In that place my wife and I would be exposed for the first time to the principles of godly living that would revolutionize our lives and set the tone for our family and our life ministry.

As I said, it has now been twenty years since I entered the real world. Now I stand at the corner of the past and present.

In one direction I'm looking back at my travels since I left home to establish myself as an adult. Looking the other way I envision the next twenty years for those of my children who are on the verge of leaving the nest. I want it to be much different for them.

To compare the life of my children with the life I lived for my first eighteen years is to do a study in contrasts. I burned my brains out on television, my children have never had one. I went to public school, my children have been taught at home since kindergarten. I seldom went to church or heard God mentioned in a relevant sense, my children have grown up in an unapologetically Christian home. I weasled out of work and responsibility, my wife has taught my children to function as part of the team. And on and on the list could go.

One thing that I did have in common with my children was a faithful mother. Mom and I were about as different as people could be. She was and is the one of the most hard-working people I've ever met and that was a main difference right there. She couldn't stand to let a minute go by without producing something, whereas to me work was just another four-letter word. During my high school years when Mom was paying the bills alone my memories of her were of perpetual motion. She was out the door on her way to work before I got my eyes open in the morning and I had been goofing off for an hour or so before she got home in the afternoon. Then straight to the kitchen she'd go to cook supper, and it wasn't TV dinners that we ate either but honest-to-goodness meat-and-potatoes meals. On Saturdays she'd be out the door early to do her banking, grocery shopping and other errands then she'd be home again and have the washing machine smoking while she scrubbed or dusted or ran the vacuum. And if I wasn't careful to be out of harm's way she'd have me in the middle of all that insanity as well. My mom. I never saw her hands idle and, small though she was, the windows rattled with the force of her steps as she strode down the hall from one task to another. If I had her energy I'd be rich.

I now find myself at the point in life when I think a lot about what I want to see happen in the lives of my children before they leave the nest. Of course I want life to be better for them than it was for me with all my spiritual conflicts and that's already a cinch in my opinion. But there are a number of other things that seem important to me and which I hope I will feel comfortable about when the time comes for lift-off.

The first consideration for most parents in launching their children into the world is a source of income. For a Christian that shouldn't be at the very top of the list, but I decided long ago that each of my sons would learn a trade before they left my home. As you've read, the task of making a living was one of the biggest problems I faced as a young man and I swore that none of my sons would ever reach adult responsibilities without a means of supporting himself and his family. In this I've so far been successful. My three oldest sons are all at the point in their trade skills that they could get a job if they needed one. This has come about simply by having them with me as much as possible as I went about making my living and teaching them as we went.

An advantage of the way the Lord has worked things out in my business is that the boys have seen me both in times of success and in times of failure. They can remember when I didn't have a healthy business established and had to scramble to get enough work. They saw the days when I was collecting the names and phone numbers of builders from area phone books, job site signs and the sides of trucks around town and then wearing out the phone lines seeking work. They have learned a respect for the seasons, too because they have seen business slow down every winter as it usually does in the construction business.

The lessons they have learned outside their specific job skills have been just as important. They have seen me lose money to an unscrupulous customer so they know not to be too trusting of people. They have learned some good communication and negotiation skills. They have learned something about getting new customers and keeping them through honest treatment and good service. They have learned that they had better stay organized and that too much work can be worse than not enough.

Most of the lessons they have learned in my business overlap so as to be valuable in any business as well as other areas of life. Honesty, diligence, orderliness and prudence will serve them well whether they are brain surgeons or paper boys. It hasn't always been easy for my sons to play the part they have in the family business but the character and knowledge they have developed through their work will serve them well and I wish I had grown up more as they did.

Along with the skills of earning money I hope my boys have learned how to manage it. A fool and his money are soon parted and it doesn't do much good to get it if you don't know how to use it wisely. I think it's important for children to earn money of their own even if they can't be about their father's business. They need to learn how to get it, give it, keep it and use it. I have a daughter who loves to give but unfortunately doesn't seem to have much understanding of how to keep. She's just little still so I'm not worried but as I've seen these early tendencies I know what I have to work on and she will not get out of the nest without getting a handle on it.

Speaking of girls, at the risk of being called a knuckle dragger let me say that I think they're different from boys and

I am raising mine differently. Proverbs 31 absolutely shows that a woman can work and earn money in business. The virtuous woman depicted there works, does business in the marketplace, deals with customers, manages money, buys, sells and invests. All that is clearly authorized in Proverbs 31. However it does not authorize her to violate her priorities as some women do when they take on business responsibilities. It does not authorize her to be under the authority of a man who is not her husband (doesn't the Bible say something about two masters?). It doesn't authorize her to work in a situation of close and sustained contact with men (the workplace is where most adulterous relationships originate). In other words, Proverbs 31 authorizes a woman to earn money but it doesn't authorize her to do it in exactly the same way her husband might.

I am perfectly willing for my daughters to stay at home with their parents until they get married. I consider it my responsibility to be their protector as long as I live and if I die before one of them is married I consider their brothers responsible for them. The girls, of course are responsible to work but the Scriptural principle is that they should be under the protection of the men in the family. I intend for my daughters to learn homemaking skills and some moneymaking skills as well. But I hope God blesses all of them with husbands and children unless He calls one or more of them to serve Him in some special way as a single person. Although where we're going to find enough young men who are good enough for my daughters is a mystery to me

For those dads who aren't self-employed and can't train their children in their own jobs there are some options. First, you may be able to change jobs. That's not something to be done lightly of course, but it may be something you should pray about. Another option is apprenticeship to someone other than the father. Of course, the traditional route of college and a white collar job may be the route for your child but I think an education is lacking seriously if the young person has not had some vocational experience before college. As Dr. Raymond Moore says, a child who has spent his entire life in school goes to college with a transcript while a home educated child goes to college with a resumee.

A family business is of course a good way to teach children the ins and outs of making a living. If I couldn't make a living in my own full-time business I would consider starting a side business to make some opportunities for my children. To me the standard route of starting a teenager's work career out flipping hamburgers doesn't show much creativity on the parent's part. The typical part-time job often throws a young person into questionable company and besides, I like to see people think in terms of self-employment as a first option. Any honest work is educational but self-employment is especially so.

If I was not in a position to be self-employed and my job was too demanding to permit me to start a business on the side I would consider helping my wife and children start a home business. Something of this nature might be very profitable but if it never made a dime it would be worthwhile if it taught my children the skills of business management.

I once took a business course in college in which I was told that the only purpose of a business was to make a profit. I don't believe that. If a business makes a profit but does not render a worthy service or produce a helpful product that is worth its sale price then that business is a failure. On the other hand, if a man owns more than one business and one of his enterprises doesn't make a profit, or if he makes his living working for someone else but operates a side business which doesn't make a profit, the profitless venture can't necessarily be said to be a failure. If a business provides a service or product that is honoring to God (as opposed to something like tobacco) and provides educational opportunities to the owner's children it is a success if that is why it was started. Of course most home businesses make some profit even if it's not enough to pay the family bills.

Our daughter Katie at age twelve now has her own business in the form of a newsletter she created called *Magaletter.* I heartily approve of the venture even though it makes it a little hard for me to get on the computer at times. Kate writes articles for the publication, edits articles submitted by other children, does the layout, types the text and handles the subscriptions. It won't be long before she's a tremendous help in our fledgling home education service.

To teach your child a trade or business should not be seen as a life sentence. I doubt seriously that any of my boys will perpetuate Boyer Drywall for the next twenty years. A trade or business should be seen as a springboard, a ticket to the future. It is a means by which a young man can earn the money in his teens to move in a different direction in his twenties if God so directs. Or, a trade can be a means of simply making a living to free the individual to work unpaid in a ministry. It may not be glamorous but tent making was good enough for the Apostle Paul.

Because of my bad start and the size of my family's financial need I haven't been able to launch my sons into their own careers as early as I would have liked. I had in mind to have them trained in a trade by age sixteen (which I've been able to do with my two eldest thus far) and turn them loose until around age twenty or so to earn as much as they could while still living at home with Pop paying the bills. That way they could save their money and have a hundred thousand or so in the bank by their early twenties to finance them in starting a business of their choice, marrying and acquiring a home of their own, getting a college degree without debt, or whatever. I figure my boys have paid their dues in the family business and as long as they are being responsible I'm glad to give them room and board while they get established.

As I say I haven't reached that goal entirely with my two sons who are over sixteen. But they're not in bad shape. Rick, the political buff, has good trade skills and the equipment and capital to operate a drywall business if he needed to do so. But because he's been allowed to pursue his bent he will probably never need to. At nineteen he's county chairman of his political party, area coordinator for this year's congressional candidate and he was the county coordinator last year for Mike Fariss' campaign for Lieutenant Governor which lost statewide but won overwhelmingly in Campbell County. Rick intends to start running for office as soon as he's old enough but he's already been talked to by various people about paying jobs in political organizations and I wouldn't be surprised if he ends up as a Congressional staffer before becoming a candidate on his own. He no longer works with us in the drywall business except the occasional job to earn a few dollars or help us out of a tight spot. He lives at home and does his part in the family but I've turned him loose from the business to follow his calling. And it seems to be working well for him.

Tim, my eighteen-year-old still works full-time in my business for whatever I can give him and the simple pleasure of the work, which he says isn't much. Tim is a mechanical wonder and bona fide workaholic who gets up early to get in eight hours helping me and then goes to his part-time job at our church where he spends another several hours a day mowing grass, painting and fixing things. He loves it and thinks he wants to work there full-time as soon as I can let go of him but I have my doubts. Maybe that job is God's calling for his life; it's certainly a worthwhile service, but Tim has so much talent for everything from mechanics to piano that I want to see him explore his options more before I'll be comfortable with him settling on the church job long-term. We'll see. He has a few good years left yet.

Besides making a living, I want my children prepare to make a life. Before they go out on their own I want them to know how to have successful family relationships. I want them to be content to wait until their parents feel they are ready before flying the coop. My two young men have already stated their willingness to do that, which was a relief after the rocky start to which my eagerness for independence led me. I also want them to be good older siblings, because that's where parenthood training starts. And I surely don't want them to have to learn parenthood on the job, as I did.

Besides a healthy relationship with the Lord, my main goal for my children is a teachable heart. I want them to always be looking to learn. I want them to respect the counsel of their elders and especially their parents. Not because we are always right but because the Bible commands us to honor our parents and hearken to them when they are old.

As matter of fact, I'm not in a hurry for any of my children to leave. We're a little crowded around here, but we like close fellowship. I want it to be the rule rather than the exception in our family that the kids stay at home until marriage. That wouldn't have appealed to me at age eighteen but it makes all kinds of sense to me now. Why should young people have the expense of establishing a separate household when their parents have a place for them? Why should they be exposed to the temptations of single life? Why should their family be something they are eager to leave?

Before ending this chapter I want to take a slap at one of my pet peeves, that being the practice of sending children far from home to go to college. In Christian circles especially, it seems to be the norm to send young people out of town and out of state to get their schooling. Often this is done because there is no Christian college nearby and the parents want their children to get a Bible education even if they don't need a degree to get a job. This bothers me. If a child has been brought up in a Christian home, a Christian church and a Christian school (or better, home education program) there is something wrong if he has to go to college to study the Bible. The same books are available to the public that are available to colleges, and at much less expense. Why can't kids study the Scriptures in their own homes, learning from and with their parents and benefiting their younger siblings by the exposure to their studies? Why can't they get their Christian service experience in their home churches and other local ministries? Aren't there enough needs to occupy all the available time and talents of these young people? It's sad and significant that most churches annually pack off to college their own crop of talent. The young people, those in the church with the time, energy and availability to do the legwork of the ministry, are encouraged to leave their families and home churches to get training and experience in the Lord's work. The church is then forced to look to the adults of the congregation, those with jobs and families to look after, to supply the need for workers. Every autumn we hustle our best candidates off to distant places then we wonder why we always seem to be short of help. Parents are saddled with school bills and we don't understand why good Christian families don't give more.

An even more serious result of this transplanting is the common phenomenon of young people going away from home for college, meeting and marrying young people from still other faraway places and settling after graduation in locations distant from at least one, and often both sets of their future children's grandparents. If no other Christian writers will bite into this topic and chew on it let me be the one to do so. Frankly, I question the assumption that God routinely calls young people to marry, bear children and minister in locales so far from their parents that their children are denied the benefits of having grandparents nearby. I know there are exceptions such as those who are called to the mission field, but we need to stop basing practices of the majority on the callings of the minority. And yes, I know there are those couples who would have a hard time raising their children properly because of the interference they would have if they lived too close to their parents. But we should all aspire to be wiser grandparents than that, and if we are our children will want and appreciate our input. Having godly grandparents nearby would relieve a considerable burden for most young couples. Just the availability of dependable babysitters who share the parents' values would be a tremendous blessing. Far more than even that would be the wellspring of counsel, encouragement and support that grandparents can be both to their children and their children's children. But this quaint idea is outmoded for today's church. So children grow up without the natural access to the wisdom of the aged, parents are forced to fall back on their own resources for a support system and grandparents who have time, experience and love to spare are left to rust away in storage. Psalm 128 ends with the pronouncement of a blessing (v.6): "Yea, thou shalt see thy children's children, *and* peace upon Israel."

In Scripture the scattering of the families is listed among curses, not blessings. How strange that in our day it is by choice that so many believers *have* children's children but seldom *see* them.

Yes, They're All Ours

Before leaving the subject of preparing the children in our homes to live outside our homes let me make note of a very important Scriptural principle that is largely ignored in our society but which I believe could make a tremendous contribution to family stability in the coming generations. This is the principle of parent-directed marriage. It was when I read an excellent article by Jonathan Lindvall that I first thought in any depth about the idea of courtship versus dating. I have since observed in Scripture that the practice we call dating would be foreign to God's direction of His people in any instance of marriage preparation recorded in the Bible. Our concept of dating seems to be of trying on several members of the opposite sex like new shoes to see which style looks and fits best. It's generally perceived as being pretty much conducted on a surface relationship level until a relationship develops that grows into something deeper. Most dating is viewed as a very casual process, perhaps describable as social recreation.

Courtship in Scripture carries a much more serious connotation. We look in vain for a record of a godly man or woman who carried on dating relationships with a multiplicity of partners. Those who at some times in their lives walked close to God and at other times divided their affections among multiple members of the opposite sex (for example, David and Solomon) reaped devastating conflicts in their families.

The pattern in Scripture for engagement starts with parents directing a young person toward marriage at the right time and toward the right life partner. This is not to say that no one will ever consider more than one person as a possible mate, but there is a significant difference between Biblical courtship and modern dating in the respect accorded the situation and the guidance and blessing of both sets of parents.

Most modern young people would react to this philosophy. But most of them do some other things that are pretty stupid, too. The spiritual baggage of guilt and bitterness brought into marriages in our day by partners who have invested too much emotional energy in dead end relationships is no doubt responsible for a tremendous number of marital conflicts and divorces.

God's ways seem radical to backslidden societies. But logically, how much can we say in favor of the way we've been doing it? As Lindvall points out, the repeated making and breaking of romantic relationships is not preparation for marriage but for divorce. Where are the commensurate benefits of dating that can be offered in its defense?

Maybe God's ways aren't so far out after all.

FAMILY SNAPSHOTS
Part XI

The children were all excited as we loaded them into the station wagon. We were on our way to Grampy's and I don't think any of us had slept too well the night before.

It was a big deal to go see Grammy and Grampy because they lived over five hundred miles away on Cape Cod, Massachussetts. It would take us all day long and into the night before we got there.

Rather than eat breakfast at home and have a mess to clean up before leaving, Marilyn and I thought it best to stop at the McDonald's a half hour from our house. We pulled up to the drive-through speaker and I ordered biscuits for Marilyn and me.

We had found it cheaper and just as satisfactory to the children to feed them cinnamon rolls from the supermarket. That restaurant dining can be expensive for families the size of ours. So I eased into a parking space after receiving my order from the girl at the window and handed the white bag to Marilyn while I passed around sweet rolls and Dixie cups of milk.

We finished our biscuits and handed out seconds of cinnamon rolls, then I called out, "Who needs a milk refill?" Cups were passed from all directions.

Eating in the car with four or five children will never be a popular pastime. It makes a mess in the car and it makes a mess of the kids. A mix of cinnamon and sugar can be a real challenge to clean out of upholstery or from between little fingers.

Four-year-old Nathan was last to get refilled. He handed me his cup and I breathed a sigh of relief at the thought that at last we would soon be on the road. I held the cup over my lap, tipped up the plastic jug and poured the milk out in a thick white stream.

My shout of dismay was scarcely out of my mouth before it was drowned out by the laughter of my wife and children.

To this day I don't know how that pipe cleaner happened to be in the back seat of our car. Or what gave little Nate the idea of using it to drill all those holes in the bottom of his cup.

CHAPTER 12: DOESN'T EVERYBODY HAVE TWELVE CHILDREN?

My little wife and I have been married for twenty years. She has spent the equivalent of ten of those years pregnant. At the present time she's thirty-nine years old and says she likes that just fine and so plans to be thirty-nine again next year and for the foreseeable future.

I'm forty-one, though I'm often mistaken for a much younger man (meaning my mother still calls me Rickey) and I plan to live to be at least a hundred unless I am victim of an early and accidental death, say for instance hang gliding at age ninety-five.

I'm asked from time to time whether I expect we'll have any more children, as if people are concerned that more than twelve might be burdensome. All I can say is that if God wants to keep sending 'em, we'll keep taking 'em. Speaking biologically it would appear that, at our average frequency rate of a little less than two years, we may well end up with four or five more before we stop producing. If that happens we won't be the largest family in modern times, but I'll bet we'll be one of the loudest. We may be already.

We're at an interesting stage in our development now. We have young men who are far enough along in life to serve as samples of our work and a smelly diaper pail in the bathroom as well. If you only like children of one age group, don't let that stop you from visiting us because we have at least one and maybe more that will suit you. If you have some children's clothing you'd like to hand-me-down to us, I can promise it will fit somebody. But don't go out of your way. We're tight for closet space already.

Next time you hear from us I hope we'll be on the farm. My dream has always been to have my children grow up in the country and though my older boys are already pretty grown up, all is not lost. If we only get on the farm in time to raise half of them there, I'll still end up raising three times as many children on the farm as most people raise anywhere. Maybe then we won't seem as strange as we do now to some people. Farm families are often a bit larger than average.

We're starting to run out of space in our present digs. We've enclosed the carport, floored the attic, turned the old dining room into a girls' bedroom and even added another aquarium. As the boys keep growing to driving age I guess we'll keep accumulating vehicles to add to the five we have now. If I'd lived in another place and time it could have been a status symbol. Sitting Bull had his pony herd, I have my junkyard.

As a matter of fact, I have some American Indian blood in me through my father. I don't know how much but it may be a significant percentage. Maybe it's fitting that I ended up chief of a tribe. If I showed my Native American heritage as much as my swarthy, black-haired dad did, I'd try to find a bumper sticker like the one my cousin saw on a car out west: CUSTER DIED FOR YOUR SINS.

Our challenge for this summer in addition to finishing this book (don't forget to recommend it to your friends) is a segmented vacation. Marilyn and Rickey are taking the younger children to Cape Cod to visit Grampy while Tim, Nate, Josh and I are heading to Missouri to spend a week or ten days at Uncle Pete's farm. I'll be working on Grandad's old house so Mom can get away from Wichita more and stay down home without worrying about being any trouble to Uncle Pete and Aunt Betty. I have the ulterior motive also of getting the place painted and the yard straightened out so it will look like my memories of it. If, in the process any lost memories are rekindled I will consider the operation an unquestionable success. The boys, of course will be in the hay field on their beloved tractors when they're not helping with the milking or out checking the stock with Uncle Pete and Kenny. If they get a free hour maybe I can talk them into a quick fishing trip.

I love to go down home even though I have to dodge cow pies occasionally if I want to spend any time with my boys. There are still a lot of the old original hillbillies down there which makes it interesting, and a lot of family tradition, too. My father, grandfather and great-grandfather are all buried in the same cemetery up the hill from Oak Ridge Baptist Church. I've got a place picked out for myself there too, and I've started digging a hole which I work on a little each year when I'm there. The ground is very rocky so progress is slow but as I say I'm planning to live a long time yet.

Although the Boyers have about died out in that part of the country I've met a number of people who remember my parents and other relatives. You have to say the name properly for them to make the connection, though. In the country it's pronounced Booyer.

For the last couple of years we've had to split up for vacations because until we got the school bus we didn't have a vehicle big enough for everybody. Even now it's tight for luggage space. Vacations are a little complicated for a family of fourteen anyway. The odds of somebody getting carsick are so good I'd rather not think about it. Bathroom breaks while traveling are...well, you can imagine it if you've ever walked a very   dedicated dog along a picket fence. Accomodations aren't easy to find on the road, either. We may be the only family Motel Six ever failed to leave the light on for.

I guess our whole lifestyle seems a bit unique to some people. But it depends on your viewppoint. I heard a missionary say that tribesmen in his part of New Guinea are concerned when their women aren't getting pregnant frequently enough because it means in future years they may be outnumbered by enemy tribes. There may be other societies so primitive that they still think children are a blessing.

Actually, I think we're normal and people who don't have twelve children ought to get the funny looks. People with less than twelve must have a lot of wasted space in their houses. Look at all the money people throw away on stuff to fill that space. Why, I've seen furniture that's hardly ever sat on. Or bounced on. And shelves of books with all their covers intact because they don't get read enough. No telling how much good food goes to waste because kids with only one sibling get complacent, not having to compete for it. Why, if you don't have twelve little mouths to feed you ought to be busy every day sending the leftovers to those hungry children in third world countries you're always telling your kids about.

If things work out as I hope they will, we'll someday buy a little piece of land out in the country, say a thousand acres or so, and build a big house on it. Then as each of our children gets married, we'll carve the happy couple off a chunk of land and pitch in on a house raising. Thirty years from now all our children and some of our grandchildren will have families of their own, all right there on that farm. You may come through there on vacation some time and ask a local, "Hey, what's that town over there? It's not on my map."

And he'll say, "Why, that ain't no town. That there's the Boyer place."

MATERIALS AVAILABLE from
The Boyers

BOOKS

Home Educating With Confidence   Paperback $10.95

This book contains the Boyers' *The Learning Parent Home Education Seminar* in condensed form. They share the lessons learned through fifteen years of home teaching with twelve children. Based on Scriptural principles and containing loads of practical how-to's, *Home Educating With Confidence* is a dose of encouragement for beginner and veteran home educator alike!

Yes, They're All Ours   Paperback $9.95

The story of the Boyers: just an average family—of fourteen. What life is like in a large family and why they have chosen to live that way. Written with warmth and humor, *Yes, They're All Ours* contains the special feature, "Family Snapshots:" Pages of hilarious family anecdotes interspersed between chapters.

The Socialization Trap   Paperback $7.95

Most home educators reject school for their children partly because of the damage done to them by the pressures of the age peer social group. Yet many parents try to replace lost "social contact" by placing their children in a variety of age-graded activities that recreate the peer pressure all over again. This book tells why *you don't need to!* The answer you need to the constant question: "What about socialization?"

Hands-On Character Building   Spiral bound $10.95

This book contains the Boyers' philosophy of spiritual training in a nutshell. Scores of simple, enjoyable projects for parents and children together. Chapters: Building Obedience—Building a Pure Heart—Building a Hunger for Righteousness—Building a Forgiving Spirit—Building Meekness—Building a Strong Testimony

More materials and ordering info on next page

CASSETTE TAPES $4.00 each

DAD—LEADER IN THE HOME (The father's role in home education)

SOCIALIZATION—ALL IS NOT GOOD

RAISING CAIN —AND ABEL (Sibling rivalry)

PROVERBS: GOD'S CHARACTER CURRICULUM

To Order:

For **books**, include 10% postage & handling, minimum $2.50. For **cassettes**, enclose 10% postage & handling, minimum $1.50. Virginia residents add 4.5% sales tax. Outside U.S., add 15%, minimum $4.00, **U.S. funds**.

Make checks payable to:

THE LEARNING PARENT
Rt. 3, Box 543
Rustburg, Va. 24588

We are constantly adding new materials, so please write for a free list of books, tapes, etc. Ask about our *Proverbs Character Curriculum* for children.